CRISIS, COVENANT AND CREATIVITY

JEWISH THOUGHTS FOR A COMPLEX WORLD

Nathan Lopes Cardozo

URIM PUBLICATIONS
Jerusalem • New York

Crisis, Covenant and Creativity: Jewish Thoughts for a Complex World
by Nathan Lopes Cardozo

 Printed in Israel. First Edition.

The essay "On Halacha and the Art of Amazement" is excerpted with permission from *Between Silence and Speech* by Nathan Lopes Cardozo, published by Jason Aronson, Inc.

ISBN 965-7108-72-1

Urim Publications, P.O. Box 52287, Jerusalem 91521 Israel

Lambda Publishers Inc.
3709 13th Avenue Brooklyn, New York 11218 U.S.A.
Tel: 718-972-5449 Fax: 718-972-6307 mh@ejudaica.com

www.UrimPublications.com

This book is dedicated to the memory of

Mr. Jahangir Yousef Nehorai *z"l*

A wonderful Father,
an exemplary Father-in-Law
and a loving Grandfather.

May his memory be a blessing
to our entire family.

Lily, Kambiz,
Nadine, Brian, and Daniel
Babaoff

You are always in our heart.

CONTENTS

Introduction

As in previous years, I had the honor to be invited to universities, colleges, synagogues, symposia and religious institutions to deliver lectures on Judaism and Religion in general.

The following essays were given over the last several years. Since they discuss crucial issues in Jewish and general religious philosophy, they invoked much debate and engaged the minds of many.

The first essay deals with the philosophy and ideology of the Halacha. Little has been written about this topic. For thousands of years the Jewish tradition has been attacked for a perceived lack of spirituality and obsession with law, criticisms most powerfully voiced in the classical writings of Christianity and of Spinoza.

In this essay I have tried to show that such a view is not only a misrepresentation of Judaism, but that it also reflects a serious error in the field of human psychology in general.

The second essay discusses the problem of tolerance and religious truth. How can one be tolerant of somebody who denies the truth as understood by one's religious beliefs, of which one is absolutely sure? When should we tolerate, and when is tolerance actually an intolerable threat to human freedom? I have tried to bring some clarity to this matter by showing that tolerance is deeply rooted in the Jewish tradition, but that this very tradition teaches us that tolerance cannot always be the final arbitrator in man's search for truth and ethics.

The third essay deals with the subconscious imprint Shabbat makes on the religious personality which carries him far beyond the seventh day of the week and how man's very being is transformed through the Shabbat experience. A careful look is given to the distinctive experience of learning Torah and the task of man to complete the work of God. The need to be able to stop our weekly labor is compared with the need to stop the work of building the Tabernacle while it was not even completed and as such must have postponed God's indwelling in the world.

The fourth essay discusses the crisis of Jewish Identity and has a critical look at Jean Paul Sartre's well known definition of Anti-Semitism. A rabbinical understanding of authenticity and Moshe's struggle for his own identity when confronting God at the burning bush is carefully considered in relationship with the loss of Jewish identity in our own times.

The fifth essay looks at a most unusual insight of some of the great Jewish Torah commentators who are of the opinion that if not for the sin of the Golden Calf the very essence of Judaism would have been drastically different from the way we know it for thousand of years. At the same it discusses why the earliest Israelites like Avraham, Yitzchak and Yaacov did not receive the Torah and why there was apparently no need for this.

The sixth essay focuses on the need to restore authenticity in religious living. It tries to invoke the need for wonder and amazement as one of the foundations of real living. It has a critical look at the belief that science has the answer to all our existential questions. The need to engage the future and to stay conscious that life means change is considered in relationship to law and the radical change in Jewish history in modern times. Finally the place of *psak halacha* as a religious experience is considered with a broader view on the mission of the Jewish people and Jewish philosophy.

The final essay deals with the question of the extent to which Halacha facilitates a greater awareness of wonder. Since the art of amazement is the very core of religious life, how can Jewish law with its emphasis on external deeds ever achieve these goals? One of the basic concepts of Judaism is that external deeds create inner mentality, but how does this work and what are the mechanics? In this essay, the question of how a person can deserve even the most simple gifts of life is set in context of a broader understanding of halachic observance.

I had the merit to sit at the feet of great Jewish and non-Jewish teachers. Besides the fact that they introduced me to the world of the Talmud, Jewish Law, Jewish and general philosophy, I had the opportunity to get acquainted with their writings, thoughts and weltanschauung which greatly influenced me. Much of their thoughts found their ways into these essays. Due to the plethora of ideas which they planted in my mind, it became impossible to mention everyone separately or trace these thoughts back to their original sources. While I take full responsibility for the content of these essays, I would like to thank all my mentors for giving me the knowledge which made the ideas expressed in this book possible.

Acknowledgments

This book is dedicated to the memory of Mr. Jahangir Yousef Nehorai *z"l* father and father in law of my dear friends Lily and Kam Babaoff from Los Angeles. It was the Babaoff family who made the publication of this book possible. Special thanks to my dear friend Rabbi Moshe Benzaquen of Los Angeles who introduced me to family Babaoff.

As in my former books, I would like to thank my dear wife, my children, children in law, grandchildren, my mother and mother in law, my brother and his family, Reverend Abraham and Irma Lopes Cardozo for all their help.

This is the first book which I have published after the passing away of my dear friend Aron Spijer *z"l* of The Hague, Holland. He was the great supporter, together with my father Jacob Lopes Cardozo *z"l*, of much of my work and books. May his wife Bep Spijer Nieweg be blessed.

Special thanks to my dear friend Rabbi Francis Nataf, my secretary Mrs. Esther Peterman, Jeanne Arenstein, the staff of the David Cardozo Academy, the Cardozo School Board members in Los Angeles and all my good friends and students who have inspired me throughout all the years and encouraged me to continue to teach and write.

The lectures were transcribed and edited by a fine group of people: Amy Heavenrich, Gavin Enoch and Jake Greenberg, each adding to the quality of the essays. To them, *Chazak uBaruch!*

Last but not least I want to thank Tzvi Mauer of Urim Publications who was again prepared to publish my thoughts.

May the Lord of the Universe bless all the above together with all those who live in the Holy Land and all men and women in our world who love their fellow men and hold human dignity high.

Above all thanks to the Holy One blessed be He who again gave me the opportunity to write about His Word and World.

Nathan Lopes Cardozo
The Holy City of Jerusalem
Nisan 5765
April 2005

Chapter 1

HALACHA AS SYMPHONY

THE STORY IS TOLD of a young Talmudic scholar who upon completing the entire Talmud for the third time enthusiastically ran to tell his teacher the good news. "Rabbi," he announced proudly, "I've just been through the whole Talmud for the third time." "Wonderful," replied his teacher, "but let me ask you one question. How many times has the Talmud been through you?"

I would like to suggest that within this innocent story lies the entire tension of being Jewish in the modern world.

We all know that Jewish religious life is defined by observance of the Halacha, a set of rules that dictates to us the do's and don'ts of our behavior. The scope of Jewish law covers every aspect of life from business to diet to interpersonal relations. And while the Jewish tradition definitely includes certain articles of faith, nevertheless the one whom we call the religious Jew is the one who lives – or at least tries to live – by all the rules and regulations of Jewish law. A person may feel proud to be Jewish, he may relate to Judaism culturally, or he may find intellectual stimulation in certain aspects of the Jewish tradition, but to act Jewishly always boils down to one thing: observing the Halacha.

The problem is that many of us may feel it a mistake to so narrowly circumscribe our religion in this way. Why, after all, does being a religious Jew have to be defined by observance of Jewish law? Many people feel a spiritual tendency and would like to consider themselves religious, however the limitations of Jewish law seem to them to run counter to any notion of spirituality. What happened to all the lofty emotional and spiritual elements of Man that religion is supposed to help us experience? There appears to be little emphasis on emotive expression, on the contemplation of the metaphysical, or on delving into the transcendent. Judaism seems to glorify Man's deeds, relating not to the whole of his being, but rather reducing him to merely that which he does with his body.

When we look into Judaism we find that this emphasis on the deed has yet another major problem. The demand for conformity so much inherent in Judaism's attempts to regulate our behavior too often impinges on our modern sensitivity as independent-minded, mature, and progressive individuals with the capability of making our own decisions. We do not feel that we need to be told how to tie our shoes or when to wash our hands. Yet the Halacha seems to assume that we cannot make these types of decisions for ourselves. There is hardly a single act or daily routine that does not fall within the scope of its ruling. It is as if we are being told to relinquish our own ideas in favor of rote compliance. Where then is there room for individuality and the spiritual expression that is unique to each and every soul?

Even for those who accept upon themselves to live by these rules, the demands of Jewish law can too easily lose their mystique. The sheer number of commandments can become a burden just to think about. There are 613 *mitzvot* in the Torah, but as Rambam writes, these are only the roots.[1] Each mitzvah then branches out into tens or even hundreds of *halachot* leaving us with a codex of thousands upon thousands of laws, each telling us something else to do or not to do. The breadth and scope of Jewish law could make even the most devout feel bound by so many fetters.

So herein lies the tension. What is the purpose of all these laws? Why are there so many of them? And how are we supposed to relate

---

[1] Introduction to *Sefer HaMitzvot.* See also Rav Avraham, brother of the Vilna Gaon, *Ma'alot HaTorah.*

to them properly? Are we meant to be the young Talmudic scholar of our story who finds satisfaction in the simple performance of the laws and the fulfillment of his duties; or rather, as his rabbi seems to intimate, should we be striving for a more spiritual transformation that will make us into nobler and more dignified individuals? In short, are we supposed to go through Judaism or is Judaism supposed to go through us?

A Problem Throughout History

The truth is that this is a very old problem. Indeed, we know that it existed at least two thousand years ago because the early Christians struggled with it too. In particular, history teaches us of one man who after becoming a Christian sought to wage war on the Halacha. He went by the name Paul of Tarsus and he claimed, as many of his followers were to repeat, that Man cannot approach God through the merit of his deeds. What was needed rather was purity of the heart, absolute faith. The secret to salvation resides in the emotional dimension of human existence, claimed Paul. All the deeds in the world won't help, because God judges what your heart feels, not what your body does. Because Judaism failed to recognize this basic fact, it actually failed as a religion altogether and had nothing left to offer mankind. According to Paul, Judaism's adherence to Halacha was its undoing.

Not only Christianity, but also many other groups that sought to break away from traditional Judaism did so with this very complaint in hand. I dare say that even the Reform movement lodged this objection, and followed through by doing away with many of the *mitzvot*. The Reformers wanted to emphasize Jewish ethical imperatives, as well as the keeping of those *mitzvot* that have kept the Jewish people – whichever those may have been – but all other *mitzvot* by implication could and should be done away with. As with

Christianity, the transformation was viewed as one from a cult of action to a religion of feeling and freedom.

Spinoza's Critique

Secular philosophers have also noted this problem that seems to plague Judaism. In fact, they were spearheaded by none other than a Jew from the community in which I grew up in Amsterdam. His name was Baruch (changed to Benedictus) Spinoza, and he lived in the 17th century. Although he had been raised as a Jew, Spinoza broke away from his ancestral roots. He was one of modernity's first truly "free thinkers" in that he was neither bound by a tradition nor any particular religious conviction.

Of all modern thinkers, Spinoza is most famous for his rejection of Jewish law. His complaint however was not unique. As many others did before and after him, he viewed Judaism as a kind of religious behaviorism that idolizes outward action at the expense of inner devotion. He lamented that the ultimate goal of the religious Jew seemed to be mere conformity to the minutiae of the law. There is no place in Judaism, claimed Spinoza, for "lofty speculations nor philosophical reasoning. I would be surprised if I found [the prophets] teaching any new speculative doctrine which was not commonplace to...gentile philosophers." He believed that "the rule of right living, the worship and the love for God was to them [the Jews] rather a bondage than the true liberty."[2]

Thus ran Spinoza's critique of Judaism. And since the time that he voiced these words, almost every secular philosopher who has had something to say on the subject of Judaism has echoed his criticisms. Immanuel Kant even went so far as to claim that Judaism is "*eigentlich gar keine religion* (actually not a religion at all)."[3]

---

[2] *Tractatus Theologico Politicus* III, XII.

[3] Herman Cohen, *Juedische Geschriften*, vol. IV (Berlin, 1924), pp. 290–372.

Religious Freedom

Yet there is a flipside: there are those who have seen virtue in Judaism where others have only seen vice. For example, the modern Jewish philosopher Moses Mendelssohn praised Judaism as being not a "revealed religion," but rather a "revealed law." "The spirit of Judaism," wrote Mendelssohn, "is freedom in doctrine and conformity in action."[4] Judaism offers flexibility. If you are a rationalist, study Talmud. If you lean toward the romantic, be a Chassid. If your bent is mysticism, find an outlet in Kabbalah. But the flexibility ends where your deeds begin – your actions may not depart from Jewish law.

As we have seen, however, others read the situation differently. They claimed that Judaism offered "freedom" in these matters simply because it had no clear spiritual path to offer. Instead of directing Man's soul heavenward, it bound his body earthward. Hence Mendelssohn's liberty was Spinoza's bondage.

Yirmiyahu's Proclamation

But theological and philosophical critiques aside, Judaism itself may provide the most searing indictment of its own obsession with the law. When we look into the Midrash on *Eichah* (Lamentations) we indeed find that such is the case. The author of *Eichah*, the prophet Yirmiyahu (Jeremiah), lived at the time of the destruction of the First Temple and was the period's main seer of doom. The Jewish people had gone astray and the ultimate punishment was about to come – the destruction of the Temple and exile to a foreign land. It was Yirmiyahu's unfortunate job to try to get them to repent.

With a bitter and broken heart, he chastised the Jewish people at God's behest and cried out these words:

---

[4] *Jerusalem* (1838), ch. 2.

> *Oti azavu v'torati lo shamaru* (They have forsaken Me and neither do they observe My Torah).[5]

Pay close attention to the words of Yirmiyahu's rebuke. There is something strange about them. If the Jewish people had abandoned God, of course they must have done so by discarding the Torah. You could hardly have the one without the other. What is the difference between abandoning God and forsaking His Torah? Based on this textual anomaly, the Midrash seeks a deeper meaning to these words – a reinterpretation of Yirmiyahu's prophecy. What Yirmiyahu was really proclaiming, says the Midrash is this:

> *Halavai oti azavu v'torati shamaru* (Would that they forsook Me as long as they do not abandon My Torah).[6]

It seems God would rather have us keep the Torah than maintain our belief in Him!

Alas, the ultimate statement of Judaism: Be an atheist, be an agnostic, even believe in another religion just please observe the *mitzvot* while you do so. But if that's what Yirmiyahu was saying, then we seem to have fallen right into the hands of those who have been criticizing Judaism all along for its obsession with deeds. How can Judaism be a religion if it makes no more demand than to just do what it says to do? No belief, no feeling – just action. Perhaps Kant was right after all, Judaism is not a religion!

Be Holy

I must admit to acting a bit subversively up to this point, for in truth there is obviously more to Judaism than just keeping the *mitzvot*. It

---

5 *Yirmiyahu* 16:11.

6 *Eichah Rabbah, Pesichta* 2.

would be too simplistic to claim that God merely expects us to perform certain actions by rote. Judaism would never be so banal as to make such a claim. We cannot deny that the *mitzvot* have a certain ideology behind them, an aim to which they are driving. We aspire to achieve something via the *mitzvot*, not merely their dry fulfillment. But what is this much sought-after but elusive goal?

When we look into the Torah one goal seems to stand out among all the others: Holiness, or *Kedusha*. Over and over again in the Torah God implores us to be holy. One such case is what the Torah has to say concerning the mitzvah to wear *tzitzit* (ritual fringes on a four-cornered garment):

> In order that you will remember and perform all My commandments and you will be holy unto your God.[7]

Clearly the point is that doing the *mitzvot* is supposed to make us holy.

It must be stressed though that Judaism has its own unique understanding of holiness. In order to appreciate it, we must attempt to dissociate it from any preconceived notions that come to us from other sources. The Jewish concept of holiness is admittedly difficult to define. Like such concepts as love and beauty, we can only really tell what it is when we experience it. Any definition seems to offend our sensitivities as being just so much oversimplification. But if I may attempt a definition through the back door, as it were, I would say something to the effect of the following: Holiness is that which a person experiences when he lets God into his thoughts, feelings, and actions; when the sum total of his existence encounters its Creator. What we sense from this encounter is something of an internal transformation that brings on a certain feeling of elation and elevation.

---

[7] *Bamidbar* 15:40.

No doubt we would all like to be holy. The only question is, how do we get there? The most popular response I have heard to this question is "transcendental meditation." Now it is true that Judaism has a tradition of meditation. Chassidism and the Kabbalah hold it in very high regard. But it certainly is not a major aspect of our tradition. Nowhere in the Torah does God say, "If you want to be holy like Me, go meditate somewhere."

The Torah does however give a different instruction as to how to become holy, albeit a rather strange and confusing one:

> For I am Hashem, your God, you shall sanctify yourselves and you shall become holy, for I am holy and you shall not make yourselves unholy….

What makes us unholy? Continues the Torah:

> …by [eating] any creeping creature that crawls on the ground.[8]

The Torah is making a most unusual claim here. It is telling us that if we want to be holy, all we need do is keep kosher. Just avoid eating non-kosher food and be sanctified to God.

The only problem is that it's very difficult to see the connection between keeping kosher and being holy. Plenty of people keep kosher, but are they all what we would immediately identify as "holy people"? Holiness is about recognizing God in everything and experiencing Him with everything. In seeking holiness we are supposed to try to be like God and draw ourselves close to Him. How could all this possibly depend merely on our deeds, on such a simple thing as that which we eat? Surely the heart must come into it somewhere? Our beliefs must be of some importance?

---

[8] *Vayikra* 11:44.

Once again we are confronted by the likes of Paul and Spinoza telling us that we've gotten it all wrong. We now understand that the Torah expects us to be spiritual, but it expects us to achieve this goal through simple physical actions. Judaism seems to have neglected the crucial elements of Man in his striving for holiness, thereby forfeiting its right even to be called a religion. This is indeed a bitter critique of the foundations of Judaism, and it is not easily defeated. What then should be our response?

The Conflict Between the Body and the Soul

Let us approach an answer by way of another question. I would like to pose this question not only to Judaism but also to the two other traditions from which we have heard so far, namely the Christian and the Western-philosophical traditions. My intention in doing so is to sharpen our understanding of Judaism by way of comparing and contrasting it with other ways of thinking.

The question is the following: What is the relationship between the body and the soul? Everyone agrees that Man has both. We all want to find an expression for our soul, to feel its imprint on our being. But the task too often proves a challenge as the body attempts to thwart the strivings of the soul. How to resolve this conflict between the body and the soul is the principle objective of every major philosophy of life. How we live, what we live for, and how we relate to the world around us all depend on our answer to this question. I would like to address how the Christian, Western-philosophical, and Jewish traditions formulate their specific and unique responses.

Now, if we are to find enough paper upon which to submit an answer, we will obviously be forced into some generalizations. I do this not in disparagement of these traditions, but rather with the utmost respect for what they have to say. I certainly do not mean to downplay their breadth nor their scope, as I am aware that today these traditions cover a wide range of beliefs and ideas. Nevertheless, there are common threads, and a discrete pattern does emerge if one tries to view the forest for the trees. In a broad sense then, and from the perspective of their respective worldviews, what do these traditions teach about how to resolve the conflict between the body and the soul?

The Christian Approach

Christianity, as represented again by Paul and some of its other major theologians like Thomas Aquinas and St. Augustine, offers a very distinct answer to our question.

When it came to the body/soul conflict, the Church fathers claimed that resolution was simply beyond human capacity. Body and soul engage in constant struggle, and neither can reach any satisfaction by that which the other desires. The two will just have nothing to do with each other. In order to advance spiritually, one must completely subdue the body. Save your soul, said the Church fathers, because you cannot save your body – it is too attached to the pleasures of this world. The ideal lifestyle mandated by this outlook was internally very consistent. Christian leaders and monks were expected to take vows of celibacy and poverty and to separate themselves from worldly affairs. Since there was no way of sanctifying the body, it simply needed to be denied.[9]

The classical Christian position appears to us quite pessimistic. There is no hope to resolve the conflict between body and soul. However, from the perspective of our experience, this view is quite realistic. How often do we struggle with the desires of the body

[9] Aquinas, *Summa Contra Gentiles* (13th century); *Augustine, Sermones post mauminos reperti.*

against our more lofty aspirations? The Church fathers certainly were on the mark when they recognized that this is indeed a great problem.

The Western-Philosophical Approach

Now let us turn our attention to the Western-philosophical tradition. This time though, instead of looking to Spinoza for guidance, we will consult the man who is perhaps the father of this tradition, the philosopher Socrates. The life and thoughts of Socrates have been made known to us mainly through the writings of Plato and Xenophon. It is clear from these writings that Socrates was a man who also struggled with the question of how to resolve this conflict. He certainly was not a materialist who relegated Man to the sphere of earthly matters. Rather, he grappled with the issue of how Man is best to live his life, both spiritually and physically.

The method Socrates taught to resolve the body/soul conflict is a two-step process. The first step involves a path of intellectual discovery of the "good life," the proper way all men are supposed to live. Once the mind, the seat of the soul, has discovered this truth, all that remains to do is to inform the body about it. At this point the body will be so overwhelmed by the beauty and depth of the truth presented to it by the intellect that it will follow its advice automatically. Socrates therefore prescribed a life of philosophical investigation and put great faith in the ability of education to raise Man's moral standards. The world he envisioned was ruled by philosopher kings who were so overcome by their own enlightenment that the dictates of the body simply did not hold any sway, the body having become a willing slave to the insight of the intellect.[10]

But if Christianity had been realistically pessimistic, Socrates was unrealistically optimistic. The flaw in his hopeful but rather naive reasoning is not too difficult to demonstrate. Imagine someone who

---

[10] Plato, *Dialogues* and *The Republic.*

wanted to become a gold-medal Olympic swimmer but had never before stepped foot into a pool. Socrates' advice would probably be to tell him to go to a university, not to its pool but to its library. "Learn as much as you can about swimming," Socrates would tell him. "Really become an expert in the subject, and then inform your body about it." Now imagine that our friend proceeded to follow Socrates' advice, earning his B.A. in doggy paddling, then going on to do his master's in advanced breaststroke. Ultimately he defends his doctoral thesis entitled, "Sink or Swim: Toward a new theory of recreational buoyancy." Can you imagine what would happen when our professor of swimming actually gets into the pool? He is more likely to drown than he is to win any race!

Training our body to do that which our mind knows to be true is unfortunately not as easy as Socrates made it out to be. The most convincing argument will always fail to move the stubborn sinner, because we do not automatically do what is right just because we know it to be so. The body, with all its complex drives and desires, offers strong resistance to the counsel of the soul.

The Jewish Approach

Judaism's response to both these traditions is to tell them that they are both right, yet at the same time, both wrong.[11] The truth lies somewhere between the two extremes advanced by the Church fathers and Socrates. Judaism agrees with Christianity that the struggle between body and soul is very problematic; however it is not hopelessly insoluble. But whereas Western philosophy maintains that we can easily resolve this conflict, Judaism counters that it is not quite so easy. The task of training the body in the ways of the soul, of sanctifying the body and its desires, presents perhaps the most

[11] For further explanation, see Eliezer Berkovits, *God, Man, and History* (New York: Jonathan David, 1959), chs. 11–12.

difficult challenge known to Man. It may indeed take an entire lifetime to achieve, but it is not impossible.

What then is Judaism's answer to this dilemma? If it can indeed be done, how do we make the body receptive to the conditioning of the soul? Judaism claims, first of all, that the body and the soul are not completely separate entities. Man consists rather of a composite of the two, in which it is difficult to tell where one ends and the other begins. The body and the soul constantly interact with each other. Therefore, whatever Man thinks or feels will be reflected in his actions, and everything that man does will influence his thoughts and emotions.

It is this latter point that is most crucial for understanding how Man works. How do actions influence the spirit? The idea here is that external movements awaken the internal ones. Our deeds create a mentality, they infiltrate our subconscious mind in ways that ultimately shape who we are to become. Whereas good intentions and nice feelings will not necessarily produce morally correct behavior, if you do the right thing you will eventually come to feel the right feelings and think the right thoughts.

The reason why Judaism stresses the importance of law, and places so much emphasis on the conformity of action, is not because it believes Man's deeds to be the sum total of his existence, but rather because his deeds are the key to all the other facets of his being. As the Torah makes clear when it tells us, "You are to know this day and return it upon your heart that God exists,"[12] spiritual growth only starts with intellectual realization, but it does not end there. What we experience is a process of "becoming real" with our knowledge, of truly making it a part of us. That transformation only comes about through one way: action.

---

[12] *Devarim* 4:39.

Spiritual Change Through Physical Action

Once on a visit to America, as I was sitting in my hotel lobby minding my own business, I was approached by two men who wanted to know if I was a rabbi. Then without asking for any further credentials, they proceeded to tell me their story. The two men were Vietnam War veterans and they had a question that they wanted to ask specifically to a rabbi, because so far no one else had been able to help them.

It seemed the two men had been raised in America with strong Christian values, particularly as regards the sanctity of human life. As they were growing up they had never thought of hurting a fellow human being. Certainly they never dreamed of ever killing anyone. So you can imagine their fright when upon being sent into war in Vietnam, they were given orders to kill the enemy. Nothing could have been so incongruous with their upbringing or so repulsive to their very nature.

At first they resisted their orders. But under the duress of their commanding officers they were eventually forced to comply. The first time it was torture for their souls. The cognitive dissonance rang in their ears as they saw their most precious values shattered before them. They felt they would never be able to live with themselves again. But after a short while the killing got easier. Too easy. Even enjoyable. Things deteriorated to the point that murder became a game to them. They would even have competitions to see who could kill the most. Such had become the depths of their depravity and degradation.

As they stood before me they admitted with heavy hearts that they had lost all feeling for the sanctity of human life. The sensitivity they had felt in their youth toward others had not returned to them once they had reentered civilization. They admitted to me that on a whim they could kill anybody on the street and not feel an ounce of regret.

What they wanted me to tell them was how to get that feeling back, the feeling that life is holy and not to be violated. They felt they had lost something and did not know how to go about finding it. Their spiritual leaders and psychologists had not been able to help them – could I?

I did not give them Socrates' advice. All the books on philosophy, psychology, and poetry would not help to regain that feeling of compassion. Neither did I tell them that their mission was hopeless. I gave them rather the advice of the Torah. I told them to get involved with helping others, to do acts of loving kindness, what we call *chessed.* "Volunteer in a hospital or an old age home," I advised. "Just start *doing* things for others and you will slowly begin to recognize life's sanctity once more. The deeds will create a new mentality and bring out the thoughts and emotions that you did not even know were hiding there."

Had they continued to resist as at first, perhaps these men could have maintained their moral clarity, even within that diabolical situation. But as soon as one allows his actions to lead him, and all the more so if one fails to recognize them in the first place, he cannot avoid being influenced by them. The only answer I could offer these men was to try to reverse the process that they had already undergone. Actions had desensitized them, and only by action could they regain what was lost. I have no idea whether or not they followed my counsel. I never heard from them again. But regardless, the advice was sound.

After One's Actions is the Heart Drawn

The same is true of all *mitzvot*, not just *chessed*. Performing a mitzvah is not merely a religious rite or a symbolic act. When we do the *mitzvot* we become them. If at the outset the heart and the mind are not engaged, by doing the actions one will arouse the appropriate thoughts and feelings. These acts slowly begin to mold our consciousness around the ideas that they seek to impart. Each act closes the gap between what we are supposed to do and that which we are supposed to be.

Listen to the words of the *Sefer HaChinuch* (The Book of [Mitzvah] Education) as its author expounds upon Judaism's philosophy of action:

> Know that a person is influenced according to his actions. His heart and all his thoughts are [drawn] after his deeds in which he is occupied, whether good or bad. Thus, even a person who is thoroughly wicked in his heart, and every imagination of the thoughts of his heart are only evil the entire day – would he arouse his spirit and set his striving and his occupation with constancy in Torah and *mitzvot*, even if not for the sake of Heaven, he will veer at once toward the good, and with the power of his good deeds he will deaden his evil impulse. For after one's actions is the heart drawn.[13]

At first the body will not naturally take to the conditioning of the soul, but after an initial push the external actions will eventually strengthen the internal feelings. These feelings will then gain more control over the actions that gave rise to them in the first place in an escalating spiral of spiritual enhancement. Ultimately the body will conform to the demands of the soul.

---

[13] *Sefer HaChinuch*, mitzvah #17.

Internalizing the Meaning Behind the *Mitzvot*

I believe this is the message of a famous story told about a holy Chassidic rebbe. His students were so impressed with his level of piety that they assumed he must fast several times a week. Seeking to follow in his footsteps, they approached their rebbe and asked him, "Our master our teacher, how many times a week do you fast?" The rebbe turned to them with surprise. "Why, none," he said. "I do not fast at all." "Then how many times a year do you fast?" they asked. "I'm sorry," said the rebbe, "you did not understand me. I do not fast at all – ever!" The students were very shocked. Even they themselves fasted on Yom Kippur, the Day of Atonement and Tisha B'Av, the national day of mourning for the destruction of the Temple and the other calamities of Jewish history. How could it be that they fasted and their holy rebbe did not? Reading the confused looks on their faces, the rebbe began again. "Let me explain," he said. "Do not get me wrong. I certainly do not eat on Yom Kippur and neither do I eat on Tisha B'Av. But it is not because I am fasting on those days. On Yom Kippur, I just do not have time to eat. I'm too busy praying and trying to repent for my sins. And on Tisha B'Av, I simply have no appetite. So you see then, I never fast."

Most of us do have time to eat on Yom Kippur and we do have an appetite on Tisha B'Av. But why is this so? Is it not because we fail to fully appreciate the power of these days and to internalize their significance? If we truly understood that we have only one day a year on which to gain atonement and purification, drawing ourselves ever closer to God, we would hardly entertain the notion of squandering the time away with a tasty meal. And if we were able to perceive the depth of tragedy behind the events that transpired on Tisha B'Av, then we would honestly be too upset to stomach any food.

The Torah and our Sages respectively tell us to act *as if* we have no time to eat or *as if* we have no appetite on these days. They do so based on the understanding that after some time practicing to act in this way we will begin to internalize the meaning of the action. As the Talmud says, *"Mitoch shelo lishma, ba lishma,"*[14] acting without proper intention will eventually bring one to have the proper intention. The Torah tells us to do the *mitzvot* so that we do not come to see spirituality as something external to us. We are called on rather to internalize it by first doing it. Once we start doing the *mitzvot*, we begin to think the *mitzvot*, we begin to feel the *mitzvot*. In the end, as the holy rebbe was trying to teach his students, we become the *mitzvot*.

Creativity Through Control

Now we are able to understand the necessity of so many positive commandments – the actions guide us toward realization of their inner meanings. But what we have yet to explain is why Judaism places so many restrictions on our behavior as well. Granted that the reverse of our above thesis also holds true: destructive actions guide the soul toward a corrupt character. But there is more to it than that. The negative commandments complement the positive, driving Man toward the supreme expression of his own unique spiritual creativity.

When I was growing up, people used to say that if you wanted to be creative all you had to do was "let go." It was assumed that the way to unleash creativity was to shed all limitations and "go with the flow." But reality proves otherwise. Letting go only makes us less focused and more confused. The range of options overwhelms us. The truth about creativity is just the opposite. It is born not out of the chaos of unconventionality, but rather from the devotion of discipline. True creativity is, as Abraham Joshua Heshel once said,

[14] *Pesachim* 50b. For further understanding of this Talmudic principle, see Rabbi Chaim Volozhiner, *Nefesh HaChaim*.

"an emotion controlled by an idea."[15] It is the ultimate triumph of form over undeveloped matter.

I remember as a schoolboy in Amsterdam being taken to see the paintings of the Dutch artist Rembrandt van Rijn. My teacher at the time was fascinated by a certain piece of his and took us to the museum to see it. The painting happened to be a portrait of Yirmiyahu crying over the destruction of the Temple. The teacher, a non-Jew, did not discuss the meaning of the painting. Rather, he instructed us to look closely at the hair on Yirmiyahu's head. As I brought my face up as close as I could to the painting, I was stunned by how real it looked. Rembrandt had painted each and every hair individually, each strand a creation of its own. It literally looked alive, as if it were growing before my eyes.

Can you imagine what it would have been like to sit with Rembrandt in his studio, watching him paint such a portrait? With each tedious stroke of his tiny paintbrush you would hardly notice that he had done anything at all. What control he must have had, what restraint! Certainly he could never have created that masterpiece just by letting go. Only a master of the trade with an incredibly skilled and disciplined hand could have painted such an astonishing work. It was Rembrandt's control that facilitated his creativity. Limitations, far from being a hindrance, are what allow us to focus our creative potential.

The artist who perhaps most epitomized this concept of creativity was the great musician, Johann Sebastian Bach. Those who carefully study his music will discover that Bach dealt with music as Judaism deals with law. Bach was totally traditional in his approach to music. He adhered strictly to the rules of composition as understood in his day, and nowhere in all his works do we find deviation from these

---

[15] *God in Search of Man: A Philosophy of Judaism* (New York: Farrar, Straus & Cudahy, 1955), 300.

rules. But what is most surprising is that Bach's musical output is not only unprecedented but, above all, astonishingly creative. According to many, he was the greatest composer of all time. Anyone with a sound background in music, after carefully listening to his "St. Matthew Passion," will readily admit that it is probably the most sophisticated composition ever written within the Western tradition of classical music. (This is not simply the private observation of a rabbi, but an opinion stated by several outstanding music critics as well.)

What we discover is that the self-imposed restrictions of Bach – to keep to the traditional rules of composition – allowed him to become the author of such outstandingly innovative music that nobody was ever able to follow in his footsteps. It was from within the "confinement of the law" that Bach was able to burst out with unprecedented creativity. What Bach proved more than anything else was that it is not by novelty alone that one reaches the heights of human creative potential, but by the capacity to plumb to the depths of that which is already given. Bach's works were entirely free of any innovation, but utterly original.

To work within the constraints and *then* to be utterly novel, that is the ultimate sign of unprecedented greatness. This is what Johann Wolfgang Goethe, the great German poet and philosopher, meant when he said: "*In der Beschraenkung zeigt sich erst der Meister, Und das Gesetz nur kann uns Freiheit geben* (In limitation does the master really prove himself, and it is [only] the law which can provide us with freedom)."[16] Bach, then, was a "legal" giant of the first order. He realized that the adoption of a well-defined scheme does not force one to forfeit spiritual profundity. On the contrary, the defined scheme gives expression to the great spiritual potential.

---

[16] Sonnet: *"Was wir bringen."*

Everyone is Unique

The art of music has yet more to teach us about how to relate to our tradition. The lesson is drawn from a personal encounter that I had with music a number of years ago. A neighbor of mine in Jerusalem happens to be a music teacher. In the summer when all the windows are open, the sounds of his violin enter my home uninvited, but certainly not unwelcome. On a hot summer's eve I indeed find refreshment in the grace of these free concerts.

One summer he was instructing his pupils in a particular piece from a symphony by Mozart. And, as teachers do, he taught it over and over again. I listened to him play that piece so many times that by summer's end, I must have known every note by heart. Sometime later, as chance had it, I saw an advertisement for a concert: the violinist Yehudi Menuhin was to perform the very same symphony that my neighbor had been playing. I thought to myself, "Wonderful. I'll go and hear Yehudi Menuhin play, and I'll even be able to correct him if he makes any mistakes." So I went to the concert, but I was very disappointed. Not that he did not play the piece well; it was just that it did not sound remotely like the music that my neighbor had been playing all summer. I simply could not understand it. The notes were the same, but the music was completely different.

I decided to seek out my neighbor and ask him to explain this strange phenomenon to me. Was it the instrument that made it sound different, or perhaps the concert hall had better acoustics, or was I just entirely mistaken? He told me that it was all very simple. "What you heard," he said, "was a completely different piece of music." "But it wasn't," I assured him. "The program said that it was exactly the same symphony that you were playing." "It might have been the same symphony," he said, "but it certainly was not the same piece of music. You see, when I play Mozart, I take Mozart's notes and play Mozart.

But when Yehudi Menuhin plays, he plays Menuhin, and borrows the notes from Mozart."

It is for this reason as well, he went on to tell me, that someone like Yehudi Menuhin would never get bored of playing the same music over and over again. When one is truly creative, it is never the same piece twice. The notes may be the same, but the vibrations and the music will always be new and each time unique.

Lamnatze'ach (For the Conductor)

Around 3,300 years ago, a highly unique symphony was composed for an ensemble of no less than two million people. Its Composer invited His conductor into His chamber at the top of Mount Sinai. It was at this apex of history that God handed over to Moshe (Moses) the masterful score upon which the Jewish people were to play the music of life. God taught him exactly how it needed to be played, not a note more and not a note less. And the entire congregation that had eagerly gathered at the foot of the mountain graciously acknowledged the beauty and depth of this divine score with the words "we will do, and we will hear."[17]

Every Jew is a musician. We have been given the notes and it is left to us to bring them alive. If we seek creativity, the notes are anything but a burden. They are rather a guide. Which ones we play are just as important as which ones we omit. And while it may be easier to just play whatever comes to mind, ultimately one has to step back and listen to the sounds he is making. Sit at the piano and if one hand plays the music of Mozart while the other just slaps at the keys with a mind of its own, I can assure you that the overall effect will sound less than melodic. Sticking to the notes on the sheet might prove difficult, but in the end it is the only way to produce real music.

---

[17] *Shemot* 24:7.

Far from being restrictive, it will facilitate the release of the most robust creativity.

What critics of Judaism did not comprehend when they criticized Jewish law was that rules, when deeply contemplated and internalized, become the impetus of a special kind of creativity, never to be found by those who reject these very limitations. As any student of Jewish law can testify, the study of Halacha and a life lived according to its teachings is one of the most creative of all human endeavors.

The Signature in the Corner

What did Yirmiyahu mean when he said that it is better to be an atheist who observes the Torah than a true believer who does not?[18] Better to forget God than to abandon His Torah was Yirmiyahu's message to the Jewish people. But that is not all he was saying. Listen to the words of the Midrash in their full:

> Would that they forsook Me but still observed My Torah since by engaging with it, the light that lies therein will bring them back to [Me].[19]

God need not worry if we disregard Him as long as we still observe the *mitzvot*. Somehow He knows that when we do these deeds we will eventually come back to Him. It is as if we will inevitably be drawn to seek out God just by following the dictates of the Torah.

How long can you play God's music without actually meeting Him? Do you have to be a trained artist to appreciate sublime beauty? Walk up to a painting in a museum and whether or not you recognize it as a Rembrandt, you will recognize the genius of the one who

---

[18] See above.

[19] *Eichah Rabbah, Pesichta* 2.

created it. We first judge art by the depths of its aesthetic appeal, and only then do we look for the artist's signature in the corner. God saw that performing the *mitzvot* would bring out such a beautiful expression of our true selves that we will want to know who it was who told us to live by them. And once we reach that point, how much longer will we remain as atheists or agnostics?

Man's heart is drawn after his actions. What he does will ultimately be what he is. In the realm of spiritual growth, action takes precedence because it alone is the medium of personal transformation. But not all actions produce the same effect. Halacha is the musical score that molds our actions into a symphony of the divine. We may start by borrowing notes that perhaps we would not ourselves have written, but when we play them with compassion, the sounds they make will soon resonate within us. And at the moment when we start to hear the music of our own souls issue forth, there can be no doubt that its Composer was also our Creator.

Chapter 2

TOLERANCE AND THE JEWISH TRADITION

AS CITIZENS OF THE LIBERAL democratic West, we not only feel entitled to the freedom of living as we please, but we duly insist on the rights of others to do the same. And yet our own interpersonal relations seem to lack the kind of tolerance so inherent in our values. While we may espouse lofty ideals, the challenge of living up to them too often shows us falling short of this tolerance. How to relate to those with whom we differ? How to live in unity even while we disagree? How to stand up for our own beliefs, yet still maintain our dignity and show respect to those who challenge them? These are but a few of the questions that tolerance confronts us with today.

As Jews, we are not immune to this challenge. The problem of tolerance, or rather intolerance, has become a major issue in the Jewish world today. Stubbornness, infighting, and a lack of mutual respect between different groups threaten the very fabric of the Jewish people, undermining our unity and creating much civil strife. This problem is most pronounced in the arena of religious matters, where argument ensues daily over very fundamental issues. How Jewish should the State of Israel be? Should observance of Jewish laws, like those of Shabbat, be enforced or should we have complete religious freedom? Israeli society today faces a major cultural rift as people start to talk of the need for two states, one religious and one secular.

But what concerns me most is the seeming intolerance regarding fundamental religious definitions, for here the debates seem most intractable of all. What is the proper way to practice Judaism? Who is a Jew? Who are the Jewish People? Many of us have very strong views on these issues, and emotions run high whenever they are broached.

A skeptic may claim that there is nothing to discuss as far as religious matters are concerned. Religious convictions are so strong, how could they ever accommodate another view? The religious have no choice but to be intolerant. Even many religious people find themselves falling prey to this line of thinking. After all, if we're absolutely right and they're absolutely wrong, what is there to discuss? If I believe in God and maintain that He commanded us to live by the Torah, how can I possibly tolerate those who deny such basic truths? There's just no room for tolerance here.

And so it seems we have arrived at a very dangerous impasse. Clearly, if we wish to survive as a people we need to find some form of reconciliation. Many solutions have been proffered in the past, but what does the Jewish tradition actually have to say on the subject? Can it teach us something about tolerance and how we should treat each other, or is there just nothing left to say?

The Meaning of Tolerance

We must start by defining our terms, because "tolerance," along with such other terms as "pluralism" and "democracy," has become an increasingly popular word. These words are now so frequently used that one would hope that most people have a proper understanding of their meanings. Yet in fact, the more these words appear in our papers, books, and conversations, the less they seem to be comprehended. Often they are used in ways that run opposite to the very values for which they purport to stand.

People seem proud to show how tolerant they are. By "tolerant" they mean that they are very broad-minded and have little objection to the views of others. They feel that all attitudes and outlooks on life should be permitted in a free and democratic society. Hence, any and every act is acceptable in the name of tolerance.

The converse also holds true: as soon as one expresses a conviction about anything, he is immediately branded as intolerant. Anyone with a strong belief, so the argument goes, is intolerant by definition.

In reality this represents a gross over-simplification of the idea of tolerance. Whether we are religious or secular, we can all think of things that as a society we clearly cannot tolerate. Anti-Semitism, racism, terrorism, and murder do not deserve our tolerance. From a more religious perspective, neither can we tolerate gossip, bearing grudges, or baseless hatred. In reality, would society indeed be prepared to be tolerant on all fronts, all hell would break loose, sending our world on a downward spiral toward self-destruction.

Suddenly we realize that there are moral principles that cannot be violated, and that we should stand by these principles come what may.

Tolerance vs. Apathy

Alexander Chase once wrote, "The peak of tolerance is most readily achieved by those who are not burdened by any convictions."[1] Often when people claim they are tolerant, their true feeling is one of apathy. The reason something does not bother them is not because they can tolerate it, but rather because they really could not care less. As such, tolerance has become a fancy cover-up for sheer indifference.

Let us be clear about one thing: apathy has nothing to do with tolerance. We cannot achieve tolerance by relinquishing our every conviction. Tolerance, rather, speaks of the case in which we have convictions, but *nevertheless* are able to tolerate those with convictions

---

[1] *Perspectives* (1966).

different from our own. In fact, the stronger our convictions the more opportunity we have to be tolerant when faced by those with whom we disagree. But if we just don't believe in anything, what is there to be tolerant about?

The American poet Ogden Nash expressed this idea most beautifully when he wrote:

> Sometimes, with secret pride I sigh,
> "How tolerant am I!"
> Then I wonder what is really mine,
> Tolerance or a rubber spine?[2]

Indeed, most of the time it is indifference that makes people believe they are tolerant. It is all too easy to espouse tolerance when one does not really care about values and principles, or about the moral needs of society and one's fellow man. In contrast, the stronger our convictions, the more tolerance we can show when we make the supreme sacrifice of listening to others and respecting their beliefs that we deem as incorrect. But to put up with others because we could not care less about their principles is not tolerance. Quite the contrary, it is a rubber spine.

The Issue of Unity

When focusing on the Jewish scene of today, the question of tolerance has taken the guise of a debate over "unity." All Jewish groups speak of unity, and each one accuses the other of a lack of commitment to this much-vaunted ideal.

To many people, the refusal by a major part of the Orthodox leadership to recognize the Conservative and Reform movements as legitimate representatives of Judaism is a sign of weakness, and a lack

---

2 "I'm A Stranger Here Myself" (1938).

of both courage and tolerance. But while it is understandable why many are disturbed by this refusal, it would be entirely wrong to attribute it to weakness or intolerance on the part of the Orthodox.

Nobody doubts that unity of the Jewish people is of crucial importance. If the Jewish people would break up into several sections in such a way that unity could no longer be maintained, we would have indeed a most serious threat to the future of the People of Israel. Still, we have to ask ourselves if unity is the ultimate goal for which to strive.

On the one hand, there is obviously a lot to say for cooperation and mutual recognition among all these movements. Indeed, to be able to agree to a kind of compromise shows strength and flexibility. In addition, the refusal by the Orthodox to bend causes a great amount of irreparable damage. There are no overtures to reconciliation, no attempt at mutual understanding; instead, accusations fly on an emotional level and all earlier attempts to find a solution are completely undermined.

One might even argue that through some kind of compromise, Orthodox Judaism could present a more positive image. It would cease to be identified as an extreme religious movement, and it would therefore be more palatable to the non- and even anti-Orthodox. Some earlier opponents would perhaps even join its ranks.

There is, however, one "but." All the above would be true if religion belonged to the category of human endeavors, which includes matters such as politics, economics, and science. But it does not. However important unity may be, when we speak about religious matters, unity as such is not the priority. What is the priority, however, is personal conscience.

The Role of Personal Conscience

Let us for a moment examine the history of Judaism. Should Avraham (Abraham) have made a compromise with the world in which he lived for the sake of unity? Wouldn't this strong-minded man have been more influential if he had not taken the stand that he did? Avraham certainly created a lot of emotional upheaval. He and so many other prophets after him, like Shmuel (Samuel), Yeshayahu (Isaiah), and Yirmiyahu (Jeremiah), were violent protestors and refused to go along with the values of their day. No doubt many saw them as extremists, inflexible leaders who shattered the tranquility of their societies. More than that, we can be sure that many "modern-minded" men in those days condemned them for their outdated ideologies and refusal to go along with "modern" values.

At this point, it may well be worthwhile to consider a major controversy that plagued the Christian world during the nineteenth century. One of the most famous Anglican theologians of the time was John Henry Newman. After holding a prominent position in the Anglican Church, he decided to defect to the Catholic Church and later became one of its most prominent cardinals. At the time, this move became a topic of intense debate throughout the Christian world.

Many admirers of Newman believed that he should have stayed in the Anglican Church. They correctly perceived that from the point of view of reconciliation, he would have been able to make a major contribution towards inter-church tolerance; he would have been considered a most authoritative Anglican with a strong tendency to Rome. The Anglican Church would not have been able to ignore him in such a position, and he would have been able to bring both sides closer to reconciliation. But, alas, the moment he became a Catholic the Anglican Church wrote him off.

When asked why he had taken that route, Newman made a most important observation. After admitting that he would indeed have been much more influential had he stayed in the Anglican Church, and as such, could have contributed to a much-needed reconciliation, he added that this option was simply not open to him. Why not? Because one cannot put reconciliation before one's conscience.

In matters of personal conscience, one makes a choice between what one considers to be true and what one considers to be false. Newman had come to the conclusion that the theology of the Anglican Church was erroneous and had to be rejected. To stay in the Anglican Church would have compromised his conscience, and would have been as such, a sign of weakness and lack of courage.

This historic event should be of major importance for Jews when debating the question of the authenticity of the Reform and Conservative movements. Neither Jewish identity nor the nature of Judaism can be determined simply on the basis of what will be better for Jewish unity. This is an instance in which personal conscience – that is, one's perception of the truth – must be the overriding consideration.

According to Orthodox Judaism, the Torah and the Oral Tradition are rooted in the Sinaitic experience. The Torah is seen as a verbal revelation of God's will and no human being is able to reject anything stated therein. Likewise, the Oral Tradition is believed to be the authentic interpretation of the Torah text and, while open to some debate, cannot be ignored or even partially discarded. Obviously, anyone has the right to challenge these beliefs and reject them. But nobody can impugn the Orthodox for holding their ground and not compromising on these fundamental beliefs; to them these are matters of truth or falsehood. The Conservative and Reform movements have, each in their own way and to varying degrees, rejected these two fundamental beliefs. That the Orthodox therefore do not want to recognize the Reform and Conservative views as representative of authentic Judaism is not the outcome of weakness, but rather of principle. It is a matter of personal conscience in which no compromise is possible.

But, while we cannot let unity be the final arbiter, neither can we afford to let tolerance fall by the wayside. We must look for ways to be tolerant, even as we maintain our convictions and defend our personal conscience.

The Argument of Divided Truths

There are several concepts of tolerance that can help us in this regard. The first of which I would like to discuss is what I call the "argument of divided truths." This argument maintains that just because I believe something, that belief does not automatically rule out the validity of other opposing viewpoints. The reasoning here is that truth does not come to us all in the same way. Just because I see the truth one way does not mean that I have a monopoly over it.

The Jewish tradition of Talmudic debate offers us a wonderful demonstration of this principle. The Talmud is filled with the words of our Rabbis who held very strong opinions about the nature of the truth. There is only one thing: they very rarely agree. Nevertheless, you do not find them insulting each other or discounting each other's ideas just because they happen to differ. Rather, each respects the opinion of the other, even when he believes it to be completely untrue. Hence we have the great Talmudic principle of "*eylu v'eylu divrei Elokim chaim*," both these and those are the words of the living God.[3] Even though they are different, even mutually exclusive, somehow both are true.

The Midrash expresses this concept of tolerance most beautifully:[4]

---

[3] *Eruvin* 13b.

[4] *Bereshit Rabbah* 8.

> Rav Shimon said: When God was about to create Adam, the ministering angels split into different groups, some saying not to create him and some saying to create him. This is what is referred to when it says, "Kindness and Truth have encountered each other; Righteousness and Peace have met."[5] Kindness said, "Create him, for he bestows kindness." Truth said, "Don't create him for he is full of falsehood." What did God do? He took Truth and cast it to the Earth, as it is written, "And You threw Truth earthwards."[6] The angels said to God, "Master of the Universe, why do You degrade Your precious seal [of Truth]?" [God responded] "Let Truth rise from the ground, as it says, 'Truth from the land will sprout.'"[7]

The implication here is that in throwing Truth down, God broke it up into many pieces. Just as white light refracts into many colors, so too did the truth break up into many facets when it came into our world. These facets appear to us as mutually exclusive as the different colors of the spectrum, but in reality each reveals a single hue of the original light.

Hence, when we try to grasp the truth we cannot do so in its totality. Only God can do that. We, however, see only part of the truth. Like pieces of a puzzle, no individual piece gives us the whole picture. The wide variety of our opinions can be partially attributed to this phenomenon of divided truths.

---

[5] *Tehillim* 85:11.

[6] *Daniel* 8:12.

[7] *Tehillim* 85:12.

Different Spirits

The Torah itself employs this very idea when it endeavors to teach us about tolerance.[8] When Moshe (Moses) neared the end of his life, he worried about who would lead the Jewish People after his death. With great compassion and concern for his nation, he implored God to appoint a new leader while he was still alive and able to oversee the transition. Moshe called on God saying, "God of the Spirits of all Flesh, please appoint a man over the congregation."[9] This refrain, "God of the Spirits of all Flesh," is very strange indeed. What was the meaning behind this most unusual form of invocation?

The great commentator Rashi (1040–1105) addresses this question. His interpretation of Moshe's request is as follows: "Lord of the Universe, it is revealed and known before You the thoughts of each and every person, that each one differs from the other. Please appoint for them a leader who will be able to accommodate each one's opinion."

That we each have our own unique thoughts and opinions is part of human nature. God made us this way. The new Jewish leader must understand this aspect of our nature and be able to deal with it in a respectful manner. In short, he must exhibit the quality of tolerance.

In response to Moshe's request, God tells him that He has just the man for the job: "Take for yourself Yehoshua (Joshua) son of Nun, a man in whom there is 'spirit,' and place your hand upon him."[10] In contrast to God of the "spirits," Yehoshua is a man with his own singular and unique "spirit." As Rashi explains, God was telling Moshe, "Just as you asked, he is able to understand the spirit of every person, yet he also has a strong spirit himself." Certainly the leader

---

[8] I am indebted to Rabbi Dr. Norman Lamm for the following observation I heard from him.

[9] *Bamidbar* 27:16.

[10] *Bamidbar* 27:18.

must be tolerant, able to accommodate the wealth of his followers' opinions. However, he must not have a rubber spine. He must also be able to make up his own mind and take a stand for what he believes to be true.

The Talmud teaches us of a most unusual blessing to recite upon seeing a great multitude of Jews gathered together.[11] At such a sight we praise God and say in Hebrew, "*Baruch chacham harazim.*" That phrase means roughly, "Blessed is He Who discerns secrets."

When we have so many Jews together, we also have so many opinions together. For this great gift to mankind, we give thanks to God. It is indeed a blessing to have such diversity of human opinion. And by bringing them all together we can get a glimpse of God's secrets, the ultimate truth that only He possesses.

The first thing we must know about tolerance, then, is that even if someone disagrees with us, he is not necessarily wrong. He might very well be holding on to a different piece of the truth.

Potential for Change

And even when one's opponent is holding on to something other than a piece of the truth, for how long will he stay that way?

The Talmud describes an interesting legal situation. In a traditional Jewish wedding ceremony, the groom says to the bride, "Behold, you are consecrated to me with this ring according to the law of Moshe and Israel." But what would happen if he were to add the following words: "…on condition that I am completely righteous"? What should come of his declaration if he is in fact not so righteous? The Talmud's answer is extraordinary: The marriage is valid, the reason being "lest he had thoughts of *teshuva* (repentance) in his heart."[12] Amazing! The mere possibility that he might have considered – even

---

[11] *Brachot* 58a.

[12] *Kiddushin* 49b.

if just for a moment – leaving his ways of error is sufficient for his marriage to stand.

We humans tend to be fickle creatures; we can change our minds in an instant. One second we believe in falsity and the next second in truth. Therefore, even if someone claimed a mistaken view last week, he might not maintain that view today. Tolerance demands that we take this possibility into account before condemning anyone for holding an erroneous view.

Relating to Those with Intolerable Views

While all this may quite well be true, we somehow know that when it comes to matters of religion, the issue of tolerance lies elsewhere. What will tolerance look like in the case where the other person is clearly not holding on to another piece of the truth and clearly has not let go of that conviction in the meantime? What can we say to someone who opposes a basic principle of Jewish belief? Must we be intolerant by virtue of the sheer strength of our convictions, or can we somehow still find room for tolerance?

Let's take, for argument's sake, the case of idol worship. Judaism considers idol worship a cardinal sin, one we should give up our lives rather than commit. The whole of Judaism in a way represents a protest against all worship of anything other than God; the Torah and prophetic writings enjoin us over and over again to avoid idol worship and to eradicate it from our midst. Suppose, then, that we were confronted by a person who espoused a philosophy of idol worship. How should we deal with him?

Our matriarch Rachel was faced with this very dilemma because her father, Lavan, happened to worship idols. We can learn amazing things from the way she dealt with this most awkward situation.

Rachel's husband, Yaakov (Jacob), worked for Lavan for many years. After twenty years, when things had gotten as bad as they could get, Yaakov realized that he simply must leave. Just then, God appeared to Yaakov and told him to go: "Return to the land of your fathers and to your birthplace and I will be with you."[13] Yaakov secretly fled (with Rachel accompanying him), taking with him only that which was his. Yaakov did not know, however, that Rachel had stolen her father's idols. When Lavan heard of their escape, he chased after them. Upon catching up to them, Lavan rebuked Yaakov for his secrecy and protested the stealing of his idols. Yaakov, still not knowing what Rachel had done, denied Lavan's claim, saying, "With whomever you find your gods, he shall not live."[14]

Sure enough Rachel died soon thereafter, as she was giving birth to her second son, Binyamin (Benjamin). The Zohar, the Torah's primary mystical commentary, asks why Rachel was punished so harshly for stealing her father's idols. After all, she was only trying to protect him by keeping him away from idolatry. Her actions seem praiseworthy, not punishable.

The Zohar's implied answer is remarkable: In stealing his idols, Rachel hurt her father's feelings. While she may have had the correct ideological intention and was justified in removing her father's idols, she should nevertheless have been more careful about how she did it. Simply stealing the idols without her father's knowledge showed a degree of insensitivity toward his feelings. For that alone did she deserve punishment.

This story teaches us a great lesson about the extent of tolerance. Even when we feel the need to intervene to prevent others from sinning – even when idol worship is on the line – we must try to do so with sensitivity. If we cannot act with consideration for others, perhaps we have no right to act at all.

---

[13] *Bereshit* 31:3.

[14] *Bereshit* 31:32.

We can see a similar message in the well-known story of the ten plagues. Moshe demanded on behalf of God that Pharaoh "let My people go to serve Me in the desert."[15] But Pharaoh refused. After a series of terrible plagues – blood, frogs, lice, and wild beasts – Pharaoh was nearly ready to concede. He came to Moshe and Aaron with the following offer: "Go, sacrifice to your God *in the land* [of Egypt]."[16] That is, you may serve your God, just don't leave. Pharaoh was essentially offering complete religious freedom within the borders of Egypt. But Moshe declined Pharaoh's offer, insisting on his initial conditions for freedom, namely to leave Egypt. Listen well to Moshe's objection: "It is not right for us to do so [worship God here in Egypt] because the offerings to our God are an abomination to Egypt. Were we to sacrifice the gods of Egypt right before their eyes would they not stone us?"[17] The Jewish service of God involved sacrificing sheep. Since the Egyptians worshipped sheep as deities, they were sure to be deeply offended by such a sight and would probably kill Moshe and his people.

Rabbi Yaakov Harlap, a student of the famous mystic Rav Kook, points us to an obvious flaw in Moshe's reasoning.[18] Who in fact had offered to let the Jews sacrifice to God in Egypt? None other than Pharaoh himself. And who was Pharaoh? Only the greatest god of all Egypt; they worshipped him over and above anything or anyone else. So if the greater god permits the killing of the lesser god, what did the Jews have to worry about? Certainly if Pharaoh permitted it, no Egyptian could possibly object!

For an answer to this question, Rabbi Harlap focuses our attention on the ancient Aramaic translation of the Torah by Onkelos the

---

[15] *Shemot* 7:16.

[16] *Shemot* 8:21.

[17] *Shemot* 8:22.

[18] *El Am Hashem, drashot* (1943).

Convert. Onkelos renders Moshe's claim not as "they will stone us" but rather, "they *will say* to stone us." This means to say that even though they will not actually do so, nevertheless they will want to. If that is the case, says Moshe, we cannot follow through with it. We cannot offend the sympathies of an entire nation of people by performing an insulting service right before their very eyes. Even if it poses no real danger to us, we simply cannot be that insensitive.[19]

There is a significant point being emphasized here. Most people's beliefs and values are derived from the culture in which they grew up. Generally speaking, that is all they know; it is their entire experience of reality. When someone puts his faith in an idol, his emotional attachments are very real indeed. To smash his gods, no matter how fake we know them to be, really hurts. The dictates of tolerance tell us always to be sensitive to the feelings of others, even when their beliefs are completely wrong. We may disagree with someone's convictions, but we have no right to disrespect their feelings.

When Tolerance Has a Limit

So far we have tried to draw a distinction between tolerance for the act and tolerance for its perpetrator. In doing so we have found that the limits of tolerance extend farther than we might have initially imagined. But is there a limit? Surely, as we intimated earlier, not every act deserves our respect. And if so, at what point do we draw the line and protest wrongdoing, even at the expense of collapsing the precious distinction between doer and deed?

Perhaps we can learn from where God Himself drew the line, from the one episode in the history of the world when even He could

[19] Later, at the very last moment on the eve of the Exodus, God (and not Moshe) instructed the Israelites to slaughter the "Pascal lamb" in Egypt. At that point in history God primarily needed to teach the Israelites not to have faith in idols – this Divine need overrode the sensitivities of the Egyptian idol-worshippers.

not be tolerant. The Book of *Bereshit* records the story of the generation of Noach (Noah) at the time of the great flood. God wiped out that entire generation in a rainstorm of forty days and forty nights, leaving only Noach and his family alive to repopulate a desolate world. What could that generation possibly have done so wrong as to deserve such an awful fate?

The Talmud discusses this question very directly, but its answer leaves us with more questions than when we started:

Rabbi Yochanan said: Come and see how great a sin is stealing. Behold, the generation of the flood transgressed every sin, but their judgment was only sealed because they stole from each other.[20]

The entire generation was wiped out purely and simply for stealing. But, if we look into the Torah where it talks about the generation of the flood, it seems that stealing was the least of their offences: "The earth had become corrupt before God, and the earth had become filled with violent crime."[21] What were the corruption and crime so prevalent at the time? Rashi explains these expressions as references to the spread of idol worship and sexual immorality.

Rabbi Meir Simcha of Dvinsk (1843–1926), in his remarkable commentary on the Torah called *Meshech Chochma*,[22] asks a most simple question: Which of the following sins is more severe, stealing or lewdness and idolatry? The latter are cardinal offences in Jewish law, subject to the death penalty when committed intentionally. Stealing, on the other hand, merely receives a monetary fine.[23] If such is the case, why did the generation of the flood receive their judgment of destruction only for stealing? Nowhere in the Torah do we find

---

20 *Sanhedrin* 108a.

21 *Bereshit* 6:11.

22 *Parashat Yitro*.

23 *Shemot* 22:3.

stealing treated as a capital offence. It seems that the generation of the flood was punished for the entirely wrong reason!

In *Meshech Chochma*'s answer to this question lies one of the most fascinating insights in all the commentaries on the Torah. We will see that it has much to say about our issue of tolerance.

In a society that generally rejects idol worship and sexual immorality, the individual who commits these crimes must receive his due punishment. For society to maintain its values, it clearly cannot tolerate those who undermine its moral code. But what happens when a society accepts these sins as the norm of everyday life? If everyone is involved in these transgressions, there is no longer any moral voice to protest committing them. The whole value system of that society has fallen into corruption, yet no one is aware of it. Such a society on the whole becomes less culpable for their sins, simply because nobody knows any better.

They are less culpable, that is, for their violations of spiritual laws, those that pertain to man's relationship to God (as opposed to social laws pertaining to man's relationship to his fellow man). Idolatry and sexual immorality, of which the generation of the flood was indeed guilty, are violations of spiritual law. Idolatry is obviously a spiritual transgression, and if two adults agree to have a forbidden sexual relationship, this also is primarily a transgression against God. For the generation of the flood, these spiritual sins had become socially acceptable. The Torah says that "the land had become corrupt *before God*," implying that it was only He who noticed. To everyone else, the perversity and immorality were just part of everyday life.

In such a situation, God says that even though we are hurting Him by violating His laws, nevertheless He can live with it. He will not hold us fully responsible when we do not – indeed cannot – know any better. He will tolerate such transgressions, at least to the extent of relenting upon the capital punishment normally due in such instances.

Thus the greater offence of the generation of the flood was not the proliferation of their spiritual crimes, but rather the widespread acceptance of their social crimes. Not the idolatry and sexual immorality, but the stealing sealed their punishment. How is it that stealing, a minor transgression when committed by the individual, becomes such a serious crime when the whole generation is involved? How can a crime deserving of a mere penalty become a death sentence for an entire generation?

Stealing, unlike idolatry and sexual immorality, is a social crime – a violation of the laws between man and his fellow. If in judging the society for spiritual transgressions God can be tolerant, when it comes to social transgressions, such is not the case. In fact, just the opposite seems to be true. The more widespread they become, the less acceptable they are before God.

The reason is as follows: Even when the whole generation is involved, no one can claim that stealing is an acceptable norm of society. It threatens the very fabric of social order, demonstrating a breakdown of mutual respect for civil rights. If everyone damages everyone else with impunity, it will not be long before that society self-destructs. You don't have to have any spiritual sensitivity to understand that stealing undermines the foundations of social life. For this type of corruption there can be no defense, no justification that "nobody knew any better." Once a society permits the wanton proliferation of social crimes, all hope is lost. At this point, even stealing becomes a capital offence.

There is a powerful message being conveyed here. When we are all involved in transgressions that "only" hurt God, then somehow He can tolerate it. Therefore, when it comes to purely religious issues, we too should be tolerant about violation on a communal level. *Meshech*

Chochma asserts that for the desecration of Shabbat, already common in his day and even more so now, God would surely suspend his judgment because as a community nobody knows any better. But when we start hurting each other, then there is no room for tolerance. We should not, indeed cannot, be tolerant. Rather we must protest, and not only stealing but all forms of social injustice, prejudice, and injury. In such cases we must deliberately become intolerant.

Flawed Intolerance

Our forefather Avraham (Abraham) was well known for his great generosity and hospitality toward guests. He would offer food and lodging, even tending to his guests' needs personally. We also know that Avraham taught much about God and converted many people to monotheism.

Legend has it, though, that Avraham once experienced some difficulty in this regard. As one of Avraham's guests was leaving, he approached Avraham full of thanks for the hospitality he had received. Avraham told him, "Don't thank me. Thank God. I'm just His agent here, but everything of which you partook came from Him." The man stared in confusion. "Who is this God you talk about?" he asked. Avraham took this as his cue and proceeded to deliver a beautiful and deep exposition about the essentials of monotheism. "He created the world…gave us life…wants a relationship with us…" But the man still looked confused. He said to Avraham, "I don't understand. I want to thank you, or at least thank my idol. I've never heard of this God of which you speak." So Avraham explained it again, and again the man insisted on thanking Avraham or thanking his idol. And the same happened again, and again…until finally Avraham lost his patience and told the man to leave. In exasperation and exhaustion, Avraham collapsed in his chair and fell fast asleep. At that point God appeared to Avraham in a vision and said to him, "Avraham, you only put up with that man for a few minutes, whereas I have suffered him for forty-six years already!"[24]

The mistake we make with intolerance is that we think we can play God. We see problems and assume that only *we* notice them; if we don't resolve them, nobody else will. With this attitude, we deny God's omnipotence. We forget that our problems are also God's problems.

From the Orthodox perspective, the differences with the Reform and Conservative movements pose many complications. From what we know of these disputes, we will never agree. The gap is too wide. So then what should we do about it? Shout and scream, rant and rave? If we are unable to maintain our dignity during debate, we won't have any effect on the other person anyway. Debate can only proceed with integrity and respect. Beyond that point there is no obligation to say a word.

It is not our responsibility to fully resolve every issue. We should engage the Reform and Conservative, respectfully disagree, and ask God to deal with the rest. If God has been living with Reform and Conservative for almost two hundred years, then it is His problem too. Let Him take care of it.

The Dimensions of Dialogue

While we cannot expect to solve all our differences, this does not obviate the need for dialogue to take place between Orthodoxy and these other movements. Objections have been raised that such dialogues inevitably prove unsuccessful. Since the parties involved have too many ideological differences, any reconciliation is utterly impossible. This may very well be true, but it is not only the desire to find an ideological *solution* that makes such dialogue meaningful.

---

[24] Rabbi Leo Jung, *Heirloom* (New York: Feldheim, 1961), p. 31.

There are several other important dimensions that should be carefully considered.

First of all, there is the purely psychological dimension. When two people bitterly disagree, much animosity can be prevented simply by making sure they meet. Human experience shows that as long as two people do not actually physically interact, look each other in the eye or see each other smile, they often develop in their minds completely distorted images of their opponents. In such a case, an important component for proper dialogue is missing. One should never forget that the success of a dialogue lies not only in the strength of the speaker's arguments, but also in the purely physiological impressions conveyed – a smile, a laugh, the way one sits, how one looks at his opponent or how one lifts one's eyebrows.

It may even be the case that both parties will come closer through such dialogue. Each may start to understand why the other happens to maintain a very different stance on the subject at hand. On a significant number of occasions, Orthodoxy was not only able to explain its position to the other parties, but actually succeeded in gaining some respect for its point of view.

Further, it is important to remember that all forms of pietistic obscurantism ultimately lead to one's own defeat. We would do well to bear in mind the wise words of the Maharal of Prague (1525–1609) who was perhaps the greatest thinker and defender of authentic Judaism of his time, and whose words continue to be studied to this very day by many of those who believe in Orthodox Judaism. After quoting Averroes, one of the greatest Islamic philosophers and Aristotelian commentators, the Maharal writes:

> It is proper, out of love of reason and knowledge, that you do not [summarily] reject anything that opposes your own ideas, especially so if [your adversary] does not intend merely to provoke

> you, but rather to declare his beliefs.... And even if such beliefs are opposed to your own faith and religion, do not say to him, "Speak not and keep your words." Because if so, there will be no clarification of religion. Just the opposite, tell him to speak his mind and all that he wants to say so that he will not be able to claim that you silenced him. Anyone who prevents another from speaking only reveals the weakness of his own religion, and not as many think, that by avoiding discussion about religion you strengthen it. This is not so! Rather, the denial of one who opposes your religion is the negation and weakening of that religion.... For the proper way to attain the truth is to hear [others'] arguments which they hold sincerely, not out of a desire to provoke you. Thus, it is wrong simply to reject an opponent's ideas; instead, draw him close to you and delve into his words.[25]

This statement of the Maharal is in no way a concession. It is rather, as Dr. Norman Lamm puts it, "a heroic assertion of self-confidence in his faith as a believing Jew, one ready to meet all challenges."[26] Religious Jews have nothing to lose when confronting the truth, and it may quite well be beneficial to hear the views of those who oppose traditional Judaism. It could only prove constructive to re-think and re-formulate the traditional positions so as to make them more palatable and intellectually sophisticated. As Logan Pearsall Smith once remarked, "For souls in growth, great quarrels are great emancipations."[27]

---

[25] *Be'er HaGolah,* end of last chapter.

[26] *Torah Umada* (Northvale, New Jersey: Jason Aronson, 1990), p. 58.

[27] *Afterthoughts* (1993), p. 1.

Guidelines for Dialogue

We can view the above words of the Maharal not only as encouragement for dialogue, but also as a guide for how it should proceed. And while not everybody is able to confront heretical views and defeat them as the Maharal was able to do, it would be a major mistake to believe that all dialogue should therefore be condemned. Only when one's opponent is motivated by spite should one refuse to enter into any discussion. Otherwise, debate should ensue, albeit under certain guidelines. As such, we have discerned from the words of the Maharal and other great Rabbis several key points to consider to improve the quality of any discussion or debate:

1. First and foremost, personal hate must never enter as a factor in the discussion. If it does, what will ensue will resemble more a feud than a respectable discussion. In order to reap the benefits of such dialogue, intentions must be pure. As it is stated, "Words that come from the heart enter the heart."[28] Ideas transfer in the medium of relationship. Therefore, the only effective way to communicate any point of view is with love and sincerity.

2. Even if we aren't motivated by hate, we must never lose patience and resort to shouting. Doing so not only undermines our own personal credibility, but also calls into question the value of our arguments. At the point that the discussion devolves into a shouting match, all hope for meaningful interaction is lost.

3. We must try to sincerely understand our opponent's position. If we can succeed in this regard, we will be much better equipped to discern where he erred in his reasoning. Showing him the validity of our perspective will then prove that much easier. But even just for the

---

[28] *Sefer HaYashar, sha'ar* 13.

sake of sharpening our own view, listening to an opponent's claim can be extremely rewarding. Sometimes the greatest insights are born from the provocative questions of an adversary. We may be surprised at what we can learn about ourselves.

4. We must always admit when we are wrong. We have a tendency to defend to the death everything we say. But there is no point in defending a statement that we later realize to be false. It only hinders our overall presentation and efficacy. It is better to cut our losses, admit our mistake, and move on to another point. We may have lost that battle, but at least we'll have a chance at winning the next.

5. Finally, it is vital that we always maintain our dignity and integrity. Act rather than react. We cannot let ourselves be drawn into the fray of a discourteous debate. And above all else, we must always guarantee the dignity and integrity of our opponent. We must never confuse hostility to one's ideas with hostility to the person himself.

True tolerance is indeed possible for those who maintain strong convictions. These convictions should not create a barrier between us and those with whom we disagree. Strong convictions must be matched by an equally strong character. We have to stand up for our own views, and yet leave room for others to voice theirs. That is what tolerance is all about, and that is what God has shown us to be correct through the Torah and the Jewish tradition.

Chapter 3

SHABBAT CONSCIOUSNESS, SEVEN DAYS A WEEK

HALACHICALLY, A JEW IS ONLY permitted to observe Shabbat from sundown Friday evening until after sundown Saturday night. I assert though, that it should really be "kept" all seven days of the week. When we look deeper into the essence of Shabbat, we discover that its observance actually entails a complete reframing of consciousness.

Words of Introduction

In *Parashat Vayaqel*, at the end of the Book of *Shemot*, we see that while still in the wilderness, Moshe assembled men, women, and children to hear his words of guidance and inspiration. Moshe then instructed the people to build the *Mishkan*, the "tabernacle" that functioned as a sort of portable temple for our ancestors in the desert.

The construction of the *Mishkan* occupies a central role in the Biblical narrative. Also known as the Tent of Meeting, the *Mishkan* served as the exact point of encounter between man and his Creator. The word itself actually means, "dwelling place." Just as God created the space in which we dwell, with the *Mishkan,* we created a space in which He could (symbolically) dwell. As such, the various kinds of work that went into building the *Mishkan*, called in the Torah by the name *melacha*, offer us a paradigm for all forms of creative human expression – the Earthly analog to God's power to create. Just as God's penultimate creation was a space in which human beings can exist, our primary role here is to create a space for God and spirituality within the physical world.

It is logical, therefore, that *melacha* constitutes precisely the activities that the Torah prohibits us from performing on Shabbat. The day upon which God rested from His act of creation gives rise to the day upon which we rest from ours. Shabbat, "holiness in time," as Abraham Joshua Heschel once called it, represents in the temporal realm what the *Mishkan* represented in the physical realm.

Given such profound mystical significance, Moshe felt it necessary to detail every element of the *Mishkan*'s construction. At the moment we meet him in *Parashat Vayaqel*, he stands to hand over a precise guide for the architecture and construction of this most precious of sanctuaries. But before he begins his address, Moshe makes what appears to be an egregious digression:

> And Moshe gathered the entire congregation of the Children of Israel and said to them, "These are the things that God has commanded you to perform: Six days you may do work (*melacha*) and the seventh day shall be holy for you, a day of complete rest for God..." (*Shemot* 35:1–2).

The remainder of the *parasha* elaborates on Moshe's commands regarding the exact specifications of the *Mishkan,* and the exuberant fulfillment of his word by a people eager to perceive God's presence in their midst. But any true understanding of Moshe's instruction to build the *Mishkan* must first explain this seemingly inapt deviation from his intended subject matter. What essential connection exists between the construction of the *Mishkan* and the observance of Shabbat that necessitated Moshe's digression?

Moshe's introductory words came to intimate to us a rare yet vital message: Before we begin the holy work of the *Mishkan*, and perhaps before we begin any type of work, we must first master the art of observing Shabbat.

Dimensions of Shabbat

It is normally assumed that there are two aspects to the observance of Shabbat. The first six days of the week we must work, developing and improving our world. Then, on the seventh day, we take a rest from all that activity. While this is no doubt the most familiar way to understand the Torah's injunction to observe Shabbat, it nevertheless fails to grasp the whole picture. In truth, to observe Shabbat properly, we must keep it all the time.

If we return to Moshe's statement at the beginning of *Parashat Vayaqel,* we will discover that this was his true intent. We normally translate the earlier quoted verse to mean, "Six days you shall do work and the seventh day shall be holy for you," but this translation is not entirely accurate. The word used here for "doing" work is not the expected *ta'a'se*, which would mean, "you shall do," but rather *te'a'se*. *Te'a'se* is different. It comes from the passive voice and means, "work will be done."

The distinction is not merely semantic. Every word, every letter, every vowel, and even the musical notes of the Torah have precise significance and a deliberate purpose within the text. Here it seems as if the Torah is telling us that the work should simply be done somehow, in some way or another; if not by us then perhaps by others. But who else would do our work? If it is our work then surely we ourselves must do it. What could the Torah possibly intend to achieve by using the expression "it shall be done," rather than the more active "you shall do?"

Birkat HaTorah

We can begin to understand the Torah's intention here by delving into a *mitzva* of a different nature – the *mitzva* of learning Torah. Like most positive *mitzvot*, the *mitzva* of learning Torah requires us to recite a specific *bracha* (blessing) before we perform it. One may not even speak a word of Torah without first reciting the following *bracha*: "Blessed are You, our Lord, King of the Universe, who has sanctified us with His *mitzvot* and has commanded us regarding words of Torah" (or, in the Ashkenazic tradition, "to engage in words of Torah"). With this *bracha* we praise God for giving us the prospect of learning His word, an incredible opportunity in and of itself.

But anyone who regularly says *brachot* will recognize a remarkable distinction between the *brachot* on Torah and those of all other *mitzvot*. It lies not so much in the wording of the *bracha,* as in the requirement of when it must be said. In all other *mitzvot*, we say a *bracha* every time we perform that *mitzva*. However, when it comes to learning Torah we say only one *bracha* at the beginning of the day, and all that we learn the rest of that day is included therein. Even if we stop for several hours and then resume learning, we are not required to recite a new *bracha*.

The Talmudic commentary of Tosafot (Tractate *Brachot* 11B) calls attention to this anomaly and asks why in fact it should be so. After all, in the laws of *brachot* we have a principle known as *hefsek* (pausing). This rule states that any break in the performance of a *mitzva* will necessitate a new *bracha* when we come to do that *mitzva* again, even if after only a few minutes. For example (and there are many examples), when a person performs the *mitzva* of dwelling and eating in the *succah* on *Succot*, he, upon entering the succah with the intention to eat, recites the appropriate *bracha*. If he leaves the succah and returns again some time later for another meal, he makes the *bracha* again upon his return. Why, asks Tosafot, does the same principle not apply to the *mitzva* of learning Torah? Why all of a sudden do we ignore the rule of *hefsek*?

Tosafot's answer is as paradoxical as it is profound. Says Tosafot: The answer must be that learning Torah is different because "*eino meya'esh da'ato*," a person does not release his mental attachment from it, seeing as he is obligated to learn Torah all day. As the verse says, "*vehegita bo yomam ve'lila*" (and you shall toil in it day and night – *Yehoshua* 1:8). Therefore, it is as if he has learned Torah without pause the entire day.

As soon as one starts to learn, he never stops. The continuous obligation to learn preempts any possibility of taking a break. It is not the law of *hefsek*, but rather the possibility of pausing that Tosafot brings into question. It simply cannot be done. Therefore we take it as if the one who learns Torah continues to do so the whole day without stopping. And we only need to recite one *bracha* because we only engage in one uninterrupted act of learning – it just happens to last from when we say the *bracha* in the morning until we go to sleep.

But this begs the question. What is happening halachically when, regardless of the constant obligation, one stops learning? What if one actually takes a break? Tosafot seems to deny the possibility of such a thing occurring. One cannot stop learning? At first glance, this makes little sense. Plenty of people engage in all sorts of activities other than learning Torah, and still they do not have to repeat the *bracha* later in the day. So then what are we to make of Tosafot's seemingly outlandish claim?

Divisions of Awareness

The beloved Rav Yosef Dov Soloveitchik *z"l*, with his inimitable clarity and depth of analysis, offers a fascinating insight into the words of Tosafot. Says Rav Soloveitchik:[1] Tosafot draws a fundamental distinction between Torah learning and any other form of human endeavor. Unlike other activities, we cannot disconnect ourselves from Torah learning. And in contrast to any other intellectual pursuit, Torah learning engages us even when we are not engaged in it.

---

1 *Shiurei Harav*, Joseph Epstein, editor (Ktav, NJ, 1974), p. 183.

The key to understanding the statement of Tosafot lies in the realization that people are capable of more than one type of awareness. On the one hand, we have *acute awareness*, that with which we are fully occupied at any given moment of the day. If we are reading the newspaper, then we have acute awareness as to the contents of the page before our eyes. If we are eating lunch, we usually have an acute awareness of the flavors on our palate. By definition, this type of immediate, even visceral consciousness excludes one object when we are occupied with another. We can only be acutely aware of one thing at a time.

But we are capable of yet another form of awareness altogether. And that is *latent awareness.* It takes place on a deeper, perhaps even subconscious level. The realm of the latent embraces that with which we busy ourselves even while not directly occupied with it, even while we engage more directly with something else entirely.

A mother, for example, has an acute awareness of her child only so long as she directly interacts with him or her. But even when the mother must take care of other business, her child never fully departs from her consciousness. She never forgets about the child entirely; her awareness of him or her just moves to a more subtle plane. Rather like a person's cognizance of his own self – it continues perpetually on a latent level even while he focuses on any and everything else in life. He does not need to walk around constantly reassuring himself of his existence by muttering Descartes' *Cogito* over and over again, "I think therefore I am...I think therefore I am..." Rather, his awareness of self persists on its own accord and informs, however subtly, all that he does.

That, in the words of Tosafot, is exactly how Torah study works. At the time that we learn Torah directly, our awareness must of necessity function on the acute level. But when we really learn it in a thorough way and we, as we should, allow it to affect us deeply, then the Torah penetrates our subconscious and continues to occupy our latent thoughts.

Torah learning has a distinct and unique status from the study of science or humanities. Unlike those fields of inquiry, the point of learning Torah is not just to consume the material and move on once we master it. True Torah learning demands that we make the experience such a part of us that when we return to it after a "break" it will really not be a new session of learning at all. Rather, it must fill our consciousness even when we depart from the hallowed walls of the study hall. That way, when we return, we will just continue our involvement with that which had occupied our minds all along. Between acute and latent involvement, the entire day will have been spent absorbed in words of Torah.

The Never-Beginning Story

This concept may help to explain a rather unusual custom on *Simchat Torah*. The pinnacle of this festival, a celebration of the joy of learning and living the Torah, comes with the completion of the yearly cycle of the public Torah readings. Or does it? Within seconds of completing that year's cycle, Jewish law demands a remarkably strange deed: to start all over again! The idea here is that one can never truly finish the Torah. When it comes to God's word we are perpetual beginners and can never aspire to much more than that. Our problem is not so much how to finish the Book. That we could never accomplish anyway. Rather, our challenge is to mine the Torah's wisdom at ever-greater depths.

If one learns Torah properly – as Franz Rosenzweig once put it, not just as a text but as "*hearing* God speaking to us from Mount Sinai," one will never feel bored with the text. One will, rather, find oneself constantly wrapped up in its beauty, unable to pull oneself away. Its wisdom will become a mental "obsession," a fervent desire of insatiable love. When we learn the words of the Torah properly, they appear new in our eyes. When we read the text properly, we realize that we never really saw it before. So then, of course, the only thing to do once we reach the Torah's final word, is to start all over again immediately!

Precisely the same attitude applies to learning the Talmud. Upon the completion of each *masechta* (tractate) of the Talmud, one recites a short prayer in the form of a promise. "Hadran alach," we say to that which we just learned, "we will return to you." We may be putting you down for a moment, but we will be back. And even while we engage ourselves with all those other *masechtot* along the way, still you will remain in the back of our minds. All that we study from now on will be different having learned you first. Until now you occupied a place foremost in our mind. Now, we merely transfer you to a more subtle realm of our consciousness.

Whether the written text or the oral transmission, the words of Torah never entirely depart from the student's consciousness. Whether by virtue of acute or latent awareness, their holiness permeates our every act.

The Work of Your Hands

This distinction between levels of awareness is what inspired Moshe to instruct the people with words "*te'a'se melacha*," "work should be done," and not "you shall do the work." Essentially Moshe posed the following question: Is the work for you an occupation or is it rather a preoccupation?

While ideally everyone should love their job and find satisfaction from their work, it is all too easy to get carried away with it. Moshe warned us not to get lost in the activity. *"Te'a'se melacha"* tells us to make sure that the work gets done, but do not let it take control of us. Rather look upon it as if someone else was doing it. That way your mind will be free to occupy itself with something else.

And what is that? Just as Moshe explained: "the seventh day shall be holy for you, a day of complete rest to God." The message Moshe wished to impart was that only once we know how to observe Shabbat would we understand the art of how to work. The mind needs to be busy not only with work, but also needs to be deeply affected by higher matters. This idea connects to the very purpose of Shabbat: Contemplation, meditation, perceiving the awesomeness of existence. For work to be justified and sanctified, it must at some level be informed by the atmosphere of Shabbat.

We find a similar vision in the words of King David, when he praised the glory of work:

> *Yagiah kapecha ki tochal, ashrecha va'tov lach.* (When you eat the labor of your hands, happiness and goodness is yours) (*Tehillim* 128:2).

Chasidic masters, in commenting on this verse, have made a marvelous play on words to draw out its meaning. If it is *only* the work of *your hands*, then it will bring you happiness and goodness. But if, however, it is more than that – if the work occupies your whole body, your whole mind, your whole personality – then you will find neither. We must always strive to maintain a distinction between our work life and our real life, between what we do for a living and that for which we actually are living. Work should be occupation – but not preoccupation.

Careless Consumerism

And yet it is just this distinction between work and life that has begun to fade away. The current vogue in Israel toward an expanded workweek at the expense of Shabbat is especially troubling. More and more stores are opening and more and more people are working on Shabbat. This trend is not just a matter of religious concern, it also constitutes a terrible sociological and psychological mistake for the wider population, a signal of both bold secularization and unfettered consumerism.

The ancient Greeks criticized the Jews for their insistence on keeping Shabbat, calling them lazy for taking a day off every week. But while the concept of a rest day eventually became common practice to most of the world, it faces great peril in Israel. Ironically, we are trying to reintroduce the Greek value of materialism into a Jewish state that should really stand for just the opposite. Based on its Jewish manifesto, Israel should be teaching the world that money and status are not the ultimate values for which we are to strive. But unfortunately we do just the opposite.

It is most surprising that many Israeli academics and intellectuals who simultaneously push for the right for more Shabbat desecration, also complain about the growth of modern materialism. They call for everyone to maintain a more ethical and spiritual focus, yet the very institution that would accomplish such a transformation falls under their direct attack. Perhaps they do not realize that it is really Shabbat for which they have been calling all along. Nevertheless, Shabbat may yet function as a bulwark against this current trend of careless consumerism.

A Holy Shoemaker

The Torah teaches us of someone who fulfilled the notion of *te'a'se melacha*. His name was *Hanoch* (Enoch) and he lived at the dawn of history, in the years between *Adam* and *Noach*. The Torah itself says little about *Hanoch*, but that which it chooses to reveal is fascinating:

> *Vahithalech Hanoch et HaElokim va'einena* (And *Hanoch* walked with God and was no more) (*Bereshit* 5:24).

The Torah does not elaborate on the mighty deeds *Hanoch* did to deserve such an honor as to walk with God, an accolade sparingly awarded to history's most righteous men. The Midrash, however, fills in the details for us, telling us exactly how *Hanoch* reached exalted spiritual heights:

> *Hanoch tofer na'alayim haya ve'al kol tefira u'tefira haya miyached yichudim lakono* (*Hanoch* was a shoemaker and with each and every stitch, he forged mystical unions with his Creator) *(Midrash Talpiot).*

This is a most puzzling statement indeed. How could *Hanoch* walk with God if at the same time he was making shoes? First of all, what kind of service could he possibly have offered his customers? One can just imagine the terrible lines in his store. And what kind of shoes did he make if at the same time he was busy "forging mystical unions" with God? More problematic still, he might even have been guilty of stealing if he failed to do a proper job on the shoes. A worker is never simply on his own time. He has no right to spend his working hours fulfilling his own personal spiritual strivings. He must rather focus on the job at hand, that for which he was hired in the first place. Making shoes while walking with God? Far from spiritually praiseworthy, it seems a most contemptible occupation!

Rabbi Yisrael Salanter, the founder of the *Mussar* movement of ethical teaching and character development, offers a fascinating insight into the meaning of this Midrash about *Hanoch:*

> "The intent (of the Midrash) is not that at the time he stitched the shoes (*Hanoch*) was delving into thoughts of God…Rather, the "mystical unions" that he forged came about because he put his

> entire mind and heart into each and every stitch, making certain that it was good and strong so that the shoes themselves would in fact be good shoes. All this he did for the benefit of his customer, in order to give him the pleasure of having a fine pair of shoes. As such, *Hanoch* was able to attach himself to God by making himself more like God in character, seeing as He too desires to do good and give pleasure to others. *Hanoch* forged mystical unions with God because all that he wanted was to attach himself to God by mimicking His divine attributes (*Michtav Me'Eliyahu*, vol. 1, p. 34).

In order to understand *Hanoch* we must look not so much at what he did, but rather at what his motivations were. Did he make shoes in order to make money, or did he make money in order to make the shoes? In truth, *Hanoch* would have rather given the shoes away. All he really desired was to do something good for others and he found his niche by providing shoes for them. But against his will he had to sell the shoes for money in order to support himself. If he refused payment he would soon loose the opportunity of providing a valuable service for others. He only accepted their payment because the profits enabled him to achieve his true aim in life: mimicking the beautiful attributes of his Creator. Such was *Hanoch*'s overriding objective. Said differently, *Hanoch* was not acutely involved in thinking of God on the job, but on a latent level Hanoch's relationship with his Creator was the great motivator behind all his deeds.

Completing the Work of Creation

The story of *Hanoch* brings into question the place of work in the Jewish tradition. One conception maintains that work is at best a necessary evil. Really it would be better to learn Torah the whole day and never have to earn a penny. But if you absolutely need money and cannot survive by any other means, then you can rely on a legal leniency to go to work. The purpose of work in such a worldview, though, will never be more than a means to earn a livelihood.

While there is basis in the Talmud for this conception of work (see Tractate *Brachot* 35B), nevertheless it would be a terrible mistake to view this as the whole picture. If we relate to work purely as a source of livelihood, as something we would rather do without, then we have misunderstood our entire relationship with God.

In the broadest terms, the Torah defines work as living and acting in partnership with the Creator. God created the entire world in the first six days, to be sure. But unlike Christianity, Judaism maintains that He chose not to complete the job. In the beginning, God created building blocks. He made the elements, set into motion the laws of nature, fashioned the earth and all that lay therein. But then He stopped His act of creation and called in His partner to complete the work. God summoned man, telling him to view all that he had created and then commanded him with the word "*vakivshuha,*" to "subjugate" it: take the raw materials and build upon them to make the world a more suitable realm for the advancement of man's dignity. Indeed, the creation chapter remains unfinished. God gave each and every person a role to play in completing His ultimate project.

Work in this light assumes the role of a religious undertaking. Any way that we build the world into a better place, improving the situation of our fellow man, fulfills our contract with God as His partners to complete the work of creation. In doing so, we too forge mystical unions with God, imitating one of our Creator's most basic attributes: His ability to create. An acute awareness of this fact at all times may prove too difficult to maintain, but some consciousness must always be there nonetheless. Shabbat observance empowers us to accomplish this feat. The necessary attitude toward work can only be maintained if we have an innate consciousness of Shabbat's spirituality to inspire us throughout the working hours of the week.

The Real Winner

I was recently asked by a Jewish organization to deliver an address at a sporting event. The organizers requested that I speak to the winner of a marathon, to offer him some words of rabbinic wisdom on the occasion of his victory. I warned them that they might not like the message I had for the winner of their race, that they may regret having asked me in the first place. Nevertheless, they chose not to heed my words and I ended up speaking there after all.

When the day of the marathon arrived and the contest had been decided, I ascended the podium to deliver my address. I offered my congratulations to the young man who won the race. He seemed pleased at first to receive my remarks, but the expression on his face soon changed as I told him the following:

"With all due respect, I must tell you that were it up me you would not be receiving an award for winning this race. You see, I do not in fact believe that you are its true winner. Oh, I know that you ran the fastest, and neither do I accuse you of cheating, but we must all ask ourselves: who is the real winner of this race, of any race for that matter? I would say that it is not actually the person who ran the fastest, but rather the one who ran the slowest. Going as slow as he did, he was able to see more along the way, to appreciate everything as he passed it by. He stopped to notice the beautiful view. He took the time to chat with some of the spectators. He may even have had the time to examine the flowers that lined the racecourse. And yet, you and he are both in the same place now!

So next time you join a race, deliberately walk the slowest you can, see the most, and chat with the spectators, and I will give you a special rabbinic award. In that way you will be a true hero and a great teacher to all of us.

Taking Notice

I trust that this young man did not take too much offence to my words. I hope, though, that he did in fact deliberate somewhat over them, because while he may have "won" that race, he had yet to finish another. Life itself is a contest, and the trend today is to race through it as fast and as oblivious as possible. We compete with each other and we compete with ourselves. We run through life so quickly that we hardly notice it exists. The more we do so, the more we dull our sensitivity to life's ultimate beauty.

And this is where Shabbat comes in. On Shabbat we quite intentionally slow down the pace of life. The Halacha even states that we must walk slower on Shabbat than we do the rest of the week. The idea is that when we move slower, we notice more. A new frame of mind and heightened sense of awareness allows us to see more of the flow of life around us. And perception of this nature is the ultimate concern of religious life. As I have said before – and I am by no means the first to do so – religion is the art of taking note of that which is already there.

You are working hard to build something, but what? Stop work for a day and refocus on the task at hand and why it is that you strive so hard to succeed at it. We need to keep both the questions and the answers foremost in our consciousness. Without a personal renewal of the spirit, the loftiest tasks may find themselves reduced to meaningless chores, to be performed by rote if at all. Shabbat safeguards the holiness of work. It forces us to capture in our minds the ever-evasive purpose that hides behind all that we do. Ultimately, then, the way to avoid preoccupation with work is to acquire in its place a preoccupation with Shabbat.

Pan Halacha

Here we are confronted with an important dimension of Jewish law. Observing Shabbat requires us to follow many, often complicated rules, which include many details and require real expertise. The observance of these laws is crucial since all of them create an awareness (acute or latent) of the day's great spiritual significance. The detailed laws concerning how to properly keep food hot, the prohibition of separating out certain ingredients, the prohibition of carrying an object in the public domain, etc., all create an enhanced sensitivity to the fact that even the most seemingly trivial matters in life are in fact greatly meaningful, as they are part of the journey on which we encounter God.

But such strict Halachic requirements carry a risk. Once they are seen as a goal in themselves and not (at least partially) as a means to create certain mental states and a spiritual environment, they can become counter-productive and even damaging. Shabbat is not a purely Halachic commodity. Of course, the laws have to be kept, but we must also listen to the music of its inner essence, which the laws reflect and make manifest. Unfortunately, there are some people who view Shabbat-observance like other dimensions of Judaism, as "pan-halachic," in which nothing but the letter of the law counts at all. This attitude damages our ability to experience Judaism's deepest spirit and most radiant beauty, as does the attitude of those people who focus on the spirit of Shabbat without appreciating its Halachic requirements, since it is the Halacha that ultimately creates the conditions in which we can partake of the day's splendor. Both approaches suffer from a simplistic reductionism that disregards the unique balance between law and spirit.

Stopping and Starting

The Torah goes out of its way to tell us not to break Shabbat in the completion of the *Mishkan*. "While you may be zealous in the rush of the work (on the *Mishkan*), nevertheless Shabbat should not be set aside for its sake," to quote the words of Rashi (*Shemot* 31:13).

Yet, as the medieval Spanish commentator Don Yitzchak Abarbanel (1437–1508) points out, the assumption that one should suspend Shabbat in favor of building the *Mishkan* seems rather natural. What could be more reasonable than to break Shabbat for the sake of building the *Mishkan*? After all, Shabbat is designed to help us forge a connection with God, and the *Mishkan* was that connection incarnate. Why should we delay our union with God on account of keeping Shabbat? Surely one should first build the *Mishkan* and only then start worrying about keeping Shabbat?

Nevertheless, the Torah says just the opposite: you cannot work on the *Mishkan* unless you also keep Shabbat. The work will not further develop God's creation if it lacks the sanctity that Shabbat seeks to instill. On the contrary, it will become a mere job, a task, a chore. It will of necessity fall short of ultimate creativity, the entire context having been lost.

As one of the great Gerrer rebbes once put it, you have to first master the art of knowing when to stop before you can truly appreciate and understand what you are trying to move toward. It is all too easy to get lost in the work, to forget why you started the job in the first place. The tendency toward preoccupation is just too strong.

My Many *Shabbatot*

The Torah on many occasions commands us to keep Shabbat, yet it chooses to do so by various forms of expression. One such expression we discovered in *Parashat Vayaqel*, but if we turn back the pages to the previous *parasha* (*Ki Tisa*), we will find yet another:

> And God said to Moshe, saying, "And you shall speak to the children of Israel saying: 'Even My *Shabbatot* you shall keep because it is a sign between Me and you for your generations, to know that I am God, the One who sanctifies you.'" (*Shemot* 31: 12–13)

We see in this version of the commandment a rather strange phenomenon: there appear to be more than one Shabbat. The term used for Shabbat here is "*Shabtotai*," literally My *Shabbatot* (plural for Shabbat). But what exactly are these multiple *Shabbatot?*

Some have suggested that *"Shabtotai"* refers to both Shabbat and Yom Tov, which we also find being referred to as a Shabbat (see *Parashat Emor*). But the problem comes when we read on to discover that these *Shabbatot* are called "a sign." Just one sign. Surely if there is more than one Shabbat then the multiple *Shabbatot* should have rather been called "signs" (plural).

Hence, we find ourselves left with a classical dilemma because no matter how you read this sentence, it does not make sense: either, as "sign" indicates, there is only one Shabbat; or, as *"Shabtotai"* implies, there are two. But if two, then why do they constitute only one sign between them?

In his remarkable work *Haketav VehaKabbala*, Rav Yaakov Tzvi Mecklenburg (1785–1865) suggests a fascinating resolution to the internal inconsistency of this verse. In reality, says Rav Mecklenburg, there is only one Shabbat. It is called "*Shabtotai*" because every Shabbat contains two elements that coalesce to turn every Shabbat into a single sign.

One of these *Shabbatot* comes in the form of Halachic Shabbat. It concerns itself with the legal elements of Shabbat, the prohibitions of the thirty-nine categories of *melacha* and the requirement to sanctify the day by making *kiddush*. But Halachic Shabbat reveals only part of the picture.

The other less-known aspect of Shabbat has as its concern the philosophical and metaphysical dimension of our existence. It deals with, in the words of Rav Mecklenburg, "*inyan yishuv hada'at b'inyano haElokim*," the spiritual condition of man in his relationship with God. This Meditative Shabbat demands an inward turn toward a contemplative state of mind, a mind aware of its place in the universe and at peace with its destiny. Halachic Shabbat provides a basis for Meditative Shabbat, the legal parameters providing the structure within which we can reflect upon the infinite. Together they make what God calls "*Shabtotai*," My *Shabbatot*. Together they form one unified sign of God's love for us.

Meditative Shabbat

Halachic Shabbat is an institution with which we have great familiarity, being as it is the subject of so much of the halacha-centric literature. Meditative Shabbat, however, may call for an introduction. The spirit of Meditative Shabbat manifests itself in the transition from our usual, every-day existence into an altogether new realm of sublime contemplation. Such a notion of Shabbat finds a beautiful expression in the words of the prophet *Yishayahu* (Isaiah) as they appear in the text of the morning *kiddush*:

> If, on account of Shabbat, you refrain from accomplishing your own needs on My holy day; if you proclaim Shabbat a "delight," "the holy one of God," "honored one," and you honor it by not going your own way, seeking out your own designs, or even

> speaking of them, then you shall be granted pleasure by God and I shall mount you upon the heights of the world... (*Yishayahu* 58:13–14)

Shabbat is a day upon which we cease engaging in our regular activities. We slow down the pace and step aside, momentarily, from the race of life. In doing so, we create a unique zone in time, a vantage point from which to view its vigorous flow.

All activities of the mundane must by necessity prove alien to such a conception of Shabbat. Engaging, for example, in such a conventional activity as reading the newspaper runs counter to the spirit that Shabbat seeks to create. The point is to take a break from the world of everyday activity, to remove ourselves from all that it concerns, so that when Shabbat ends and we have to return to that world, we do so with a heightened awareness of its ultimate meaning. By focusing our attention deliberately and acutely on the purpose of creation for one day a week, we ensure that all our work toward that aim in the week to come will be infused with a consciousness of our divine mission as partners with God.

But in order to truly accomplish the meditative, Shabbat itself must be an experience of a different order altogether.

The Shabbat Within

The story is told of a holy Hassidic rebbe who experienced the most unusual of dreams. He dreamt that a celestial being appeared to him in the form of a man and offered to take him on a tour of the Next World. Upon their arrival, the being asked the rebbe what he most wanted to see. Anything that he might wish to know from the World of Truth would readily be made known to him. The rebbe did not have to think long as to what his request would be. "Show me my great and holy teachers. How do they fare in the world of the eternal?

What in fact does everlasting bliss look like?" The heavenly escort dutifully granted the rebbe's petition. He proceeded to lead him into a vast study chamber within which the rebbe could gaze upon his teachers as they partook of their ultimate reward.

As the door to this great chamber flung open before him, the rebbe viewed the answer to his questions. He saw all his teachers, from childhood through the maturity of his education, sitting in this study hall, learning in pairs with each other just as he had known them to do during their lifetimes.

The rebbe was greatly surprised by the scene. In a bewildered and somewhat disappointed tone, he told his guide, "I do not understand. Here my teachers appear before me just as I had always known them. This is all very nice, but I expected to see them dwelling in eternal paradise?" The celestial being answered him quickly and to the point, "Do not look for the paradise within which they dwell, but rather the paradise that dwells within them."

So too Shabbat. To the external observer everything may look the same as it does the rest of the week, but the internal experience differs markedly. When we eat on Shabbat, it is not simply to satiation but rather to give honor and delight to the day. When we sleep on Shabbat, it is no mere rest but rather the tranquil slumber of a mind at peace with the world. When we speak on Shabbat, it is not idle chatter but rather words of holiness that enlighten the spirit with wisdom and understanding. The entire atmosphere, while superficially the same, is in actuality something new and completely different.

The Redemption of Shabbat

While Meditative Shabbat certainly has its advantages, its ultimate reward has yet to come to fruition:

> Rabbi Yochanan said in the name of Rabbi Shimon bar Yochai: Would that the Jewish people were to keep but two *Shabbatot* correctly, immediately they would be redeemed, as it says, "For thus said God (even) to the barren ones who observe My *Shabbatot...*' I shall bring them to My Mount of Holiness"' (*Yishayahu* 56:4–7). –Talmud, *Shabbat* 118B

This is a most incredible assertion. Keep just two *Shabbatot* and the Mashiach (Messiah) will instantaneously usher in our redemption. While normally we understand this statement to refer to our keeping of two *Shabbatot* in a row, this Shabbat and the next, the insight of Rabbi Mecklenburg forces us to seek a deeper meaning. You see, in this verse as well God speaks of His *Shabbatot*, "*Shabtotai*."

What we need in order to merit the Mashiach is not the observance of Halachic Shabbat for two consecutive weeks, but rather the fulfillment in one week of the two elements of *Shabtotai*, the Halachic and the Meditative. Only once Shabbat is observed fully in this regard can we expect to witness ultimate redemption from our prolonged exile.

And if part of the reason for that exile in the first place was, as the Talmud clearly states (*Bava Metziah* 85B), that we did not bless properly over the Torah, then perhaps the problem is that we fail to fulfill the ultimate implication of that *bracha*. We must not consign spirituality to an isolated segment of our lives, a pastime to be enjoyed once everything of real importance has already been accomplished. We must rather come to view our very lives as part and parcel with the Spirit, inextricably bound up with the ineffability of every precious moment. Then, when we make blessings on the Torah at the beginning of the day, we will do so with an understanding that the entire day to follow shall be spent swimming in and out of the acute and latent awareness of our lives' spiritual purpose. And when we keep Shabbat too, it will instill the rest of the week with a meditative aura, infusing every act of work with everlasting significance.

At that point, spirituality will cease to be merely an ephemeral euphoria, and Shabbat will cease to be merely a one-day-a-week occurrence. Ultimately, we will redeem Shabbat, as such, by keeping it all seven days of the week. And then Shabbat will redeem us.

Chapter 4

JEAN PAUL SARTRE, ANTI-SEMITISM AND JEWISH IDENTITY

IN 1946, THE FRENCH EXISTENTIAL PHILOSOPHER, Jean Paul Sartre published his famous treatise on Anti-Semitism, Anti-Semite and Jew. In this study Sartre analyzes Anti-Semitism and tries to illuminate the depths of its ugliness. The essay directly attacks anti-Semitism and offers a "cure" for mankind to rid itself of this disease. Indeed, Sartre identifies Anti-Semitism as a sickness of the human soul that requires surgery.

The central concept in this study is that of "authenticity." According to Sartre, the root cause of anti-Semitism is that people lack authenticity, which he defines as the ability to be oneself and accept oneself for what one really is, with all one's positive and negative character traits. Anti-Semites are people who are unable to feel comfortable in their own skins, and then accuse others of causing their failures and shortcomings. They cannot accept what they see when they look in the mirror, and thus constantly focus their attention in the direction of others. In their search for a group whom they can easily identify as the source of what they lack, they look for an underdog, for those who cannot defend themselves. And so, they become anti-Semites, since Jews, over the thousands of years, have been a small nation, most of the time living in exile under very difficult circumstances that made it virtually impossible to protect themselves. Consequently, argues Sartre, once the gentile becomes authentic and no longer needs to project his fear and discontent on others, he will cease to be anti-Semitic.

But what about Jewish authenticity? To this question Sartre responds with a forthright definition: "This is for the Jew to live to the full his condition as a Jew."[1] At first, one cannot but agree with Sartre. For the Jew to live his life as a Jew and not to hide or deny it, seems indeed to be the only way to achieve internal authenticity. Once the Jew respects his own traditions and is proud of his highly unusual history – once he makes a deep commitment to Judaism – then one can indeed speak of Jewish authenticity. This however, is not at all what Sartre has in mind.

As we read on, we realize that Sartre has an all together different understanding of what it means for a Jew "to live to the full his condition as a Jew." Instead of calling on Jews to respect their own traditions and live according to the Torah, he calls for a radical re-assessment of what it means to be Jewish, and in doing so, he offers the bleakest analysis, offering a concept of Jewishness that stands in total opposition to every authentic Jewish interpretation.

To introduce his theory, Sartre makes the following disturbing observation: "Jews have neither community of interests, nor community of beliefs. They do not have the same fatherland, they have no history."[2] Sartre argues that it is not Judaism, nor Israel, nor Jewish history which defines the Jew. If anything, these are by-products – the associated sub-cultural accoutrements from a prior Jewishness. But what then do Jews have in common? What makes the Jew Jewish?

"The sole tie that binds them is the hostility and the disdain of the societies which surround them. Thus the authentic Jew is the one who asserts his claim in the face of the disdain shown toward him."[3]

---

[1] Jean Paul Sartre, *Anti-Semite and Jew*, translated by George J. Becker, Schocken Books, NY, 1965.

[2] Ibid., p. 91

[3] Ibid.

In other words, to be Jewish is to be the object of anti-Semitism and to face this fact unflinchingly. Once Jews realize this fact, they are authentic and true to themselves. This for Sartre, is the essential definition of the Jew. The Jew's existence depends on the hatred of others. Indeed, it is out of the gentiles' primordial hostility that the Jew is formed.

Sartre's observation requires our careful consideration. When he argues that Jews have no community, no fatherland or history, Sartre knows full well what he writes. Sartre does not deny that there is Judaism, that Jews have a most unusual history. As Leo Baeck once said, "more history has been assigned to these people than other people."[4] But this history of the Jews, their longing for their land and even their religion, is not the result of their own endeavors, but of the hatred of others. Jewish History, argues Sartre, just is the history of anti-Semitism. What glues the Jews together and what has made them a unique and eternally enduring people is that they are singled out for hatred. Their unique and unprecedented history and power to survive against all odds is not the result of a genuine inner strength, but merely an ability to resist external abhorrence. Sartre's is a geological metaphor. The intense pressure from without melds the Jews together, turning them into an indestructible nation.

Gentle Liquidation

That Sartre contradicts himself does not seem to worry him. In the case of all other nations, authenticity means to be one's self and not to allow others to determine one's very being. For the Jew alone, this is different. The Jew's authenticity is to recognize and accept that he is essentially inauthentic. As such Sartre calls for the gentle liquidation of the Jewish people, not out of hatred, but in fact out of love. Since anti-Semitism is a great injustice, we should hope and pray for its end.

---

[4] Leo Baeck, *This People of Israel*, p. 402.

But of course, this ipso facto will bring an end to the very existence of the Jewish people. This indeed is the only logical outcome. Interestingly, the anti-Semite now finds himself in an unusual paradox according to Sartre: to destroy the Jews all he must do is stop wishing and working for their destruction!

"Thus, the authentic Jew is one who thinks of himself as a Jew because the anti-Semite has put him in the situation of a Jew is not opposed to assimilation any more than the class-conscious worker is opposed to the liquidation of the classes... The authentic Jew simply renounces for himself an assimilation that is today impossible; he awaits the radical liquidation of anti-Semitism for his sons."[5]

That Sartre comes to this conclusion out of genuine concern for the Jewish people, and as an outgrowth of his ongoing battle against the evil of anti-Semitism, does not take away from the fact that his conclusion – although for totally different reasons – comes out identical to the ideology espoused by Hitler and the Nazi-regime: A world without Jews is a better world.

Sartre's idea that anti-Semitism provides the life-force behind the Jews' survival throughout history is not entirely new. Already in the seventeenth century Spinoza made a similar observation in his *Tractatus Theologico Politicus.*[6] Nor can one deny the fact that the Jewish Tradition itself hints in this direction.[7] Indeed, God always seems to find a way to send an enemy to make it impossible for Jews to assimilate completely. Sartre's contribution is of such great significance though, because a great number of scholars, including Jewish scholars and thinkers, adopted his approach. While early generations of Jews would never have seen their destiny and identity

---

[5] Ibid., p. 50.

[6] Spinoza, *A Theologico-Political Treatise*, translated by R.H.M. Elwes, NY, Dover, 1951, p. 55.

[7] See Amos 3:2 and commentaries.

in Sartre's terms, there is much evidence to suggest that since the emancipation of the Jews in the 19th century, more and more Jews have accepted Sartre's theory.

After the Holocaust, the question "who is a Jew" became one of great urgency. For thousands of years Jewishness was determined according to Jewish tradition. A Jew was a person born from a Jewish mother, or who converted according to Torah law. It meant that one belonged to a nation with a deeply religious and moral message. Jewishness was understood in purely Halachic terms, and no Jew would even consider questioning these definitions. But with the radical shifts of the 19th century, attempts were made to secularize even the definition of the Jew, which ultimately led to great confusion and a myriad of conflicting interpretations. This was caused by the desire to become part of European culture, to be accepted by the gentile world, and to be able to interact with that world on a completely equal basis. As long as Jews continued to eat kosher, to observe their Shabbat on Saturday instead of Sunday, to pray in Hebrew, and to circumcise their sons, it would be hard to integrate into the European gentile's world.

Judaism: Hereditary Illness?

In Israel, this issue continues to burn, robbing many Israelis of their sense of identity. Chief Rabbi Professor Jonathan Sacks quotes a young Israeli who was once asked what it meant to him to be Jewish: "Judaism 'is a hereditary illness.... You can get it from your parents and also pass it along to your children. And why call it an illness? Because not a small number of people have died from it."[8]

It is not difficult to understand how this young Israeli came to such a grim conclusion. When the "old" religious definition of

---

[8] Jonathan Sacks, *Radical Then, Radical Now, The Legacy of the Worlds Oldest Religion*, HarperCollins, London, 2000, p. 2.

Jewishness was challenged and undermined, there was no new adequate one to replace it. Earlier generations saw their Jewishness in the light of their universal ethical-monotheistic mission to bring God-consciousness into the world. It was a great privilege and an honor to be a Jew, and to live by the commandments of the Torah and its oral Tradition. But when the mission was removed from the heart of being Jewish, Judaism turned into a burden without a rational *raison d'etre*. In their quest to come up with a new meaning for Jewishness, scholars and thinkers groped for, and suggested, a hodgepodge of definitions, but none could be maintained with any degree of intellectual honesty. In the eyes of many Jews, Jewishness lost much of its beauty and its accompanying feeling of pride. Gone was the mission and the awareness that one lived by a divine covenant of high responsibility and dignity. And since there is no alternative definition of Jewishness, because Jewishness is just about our special relationship with the Creator of the Universe, Judaism for the uninitiated became a negative burden.

Holocaust Obsession

The pre-occupation with the Holocaust as a source of identity in many Jewish assimilated circles throughout the world, which in some cases approaches the level of an obsession, is a clear manifestation of this trend. While no one would deny the need to study, discuss, and remember the Holocaust in all its dimensions and ugliness, it is clear that on a deeper level Holocaust memorialization has replaced classical Judaism as a new form of quasi-religious worship. Holocaust memorial centers have proliferated in nearly every part of the Jewish world in ways that are frequently problematic. Building memorials is not in itself such a problem, except that they tend to exist in the absence of other Jewish centers that could provide a highly positive understanding of what it means to be a Jew. Memorial centers are visited by thousands of young Jews who would never enter a synagogue, take part in Jewish learning sessions, or participate in any other form of uplifting Jewish life-experience. The result is obvious: Jewishness becomes synonymous with suffering. We also find that Holocaust programs dominate the Jewish Studies Departments in many universities, and that the Holocaust is the primary theme explored by modern Jewish literature.

Although the Holocaust provides the secular Jewish community with an identity, it is a horribly negative and distorted image of our people. We are not merely a nation that suffers, but sadly this idea is what unites an otherwise divided community and provides the logic for secular Jewish survival. They persist to spite Hitler and in so doing have unwittingly become Sartre's Jews! They are Jews only because of gentile hatred. It is perfectly understandable why young Jews would view their Judaism as an affliction they contracted from their parents and which they may or may not wish to pass on to their children.

One is reminded of the well known Jewish philosopher, Professor David Hartman, who observed that we cannot build the future of the people of Israel on the ashes of Auschwitz. Indeed, such an approach ultimately leads to a disaster the consequences of which we can already see. Judaism as protest against Hitler, produced a generation of young people that despises and disregards its Jewishness. The Holocaust scholar Lucy Davidowicz warned us when she wrote that, "If we are a people that gets murdered, the young people will flee from us."[9]

The preoccupation with the Holocaust, particularly in America, may serve as a subconscious escape-route from a positive identity of Jewishness and Judaism. Once a person no longer wants Judaism to

---

[9] Quoted by Jonathan Sacks, *Traditional Alternatives, Orthodoxy and the Future of the Jewish People*, Jews' College Publications, London, 1989, p 107.

be at the center of his life, but desires instead to release himself of its responsibilities and mission, he is left in a precarious situation. Unless he is willing to turn his back on his heritage completely, he must find a justification for identifying himself as a Jew. In the absence of a constructive, positive motivation, he is forced to look for a negative source cause. In the Holocaust, he finds his tunnel out, but it is a dark and ugly passageway devoid of the joy and stimulation that real Jewish content provides.

The younger generations must come to learn that Judaism and Jewishness live on *despite* Auschwitz and not because of it.

Pride in Israel

Still, this is not the whole picture. After all, it cannot be denied that the establishment of the State of Israel created a completely different spirit within our nation. The emergence of a Jewish state became, after all, a source of tremendous pride for Jews, wherever they found themselves. In contrast to the victimization of the Holocaust, the Jewish people suddenly felt a renewed sense of destiny. With the creation of our own state, our people's suffering drifted into the background of our identity, and was replaced by a feeling that Jews working together can accomplish the impossible. The feeling that Jews were re-entering history in an unprecedented way, *sui generis*, stood in total opposition to the experience of the Holocaust. A nation that, after losing six million of its members, found its way home after nearly two thousand years of exile, and built a state from scratch while defending itself against several mighty Arab armies, was something that for many, radically changed the meaning of Jewishness.

In fact, many scholars and Zionist leaders believed the establishment of the State of Israel would finally solve the problem of anti-Semitism. Israel would normalize the Jews. Jews would be considered a nation like any other. No longer playing the underdog under Diaspora conditions, Jews would consequently be accepted and embraced by the international community. As such Israel became the "baby" of even the most assimilated Jews, and produced a groundswell of nationalistic spirit.

Above all, Zionism became the sought-after substitute for authentic Judaism. It was not Jewish Tradition that would keep Jews alive and together, but Zionism. Many Zionist thinkers declared that while Judaism had undoubtedly kept the Jews alive in the Diaspora, it had now become obsolete and could respectfully be dropped. Zionism became the new *raison d'etre* of the Jews. The Jews found a new mission and a new definition to guarantee their future.

A careful examination of Israel's history shows, however, that the Zionist ideal started to become untenable in 1967. While Israel had been an unprecedented success story in its early days, the cracks in its walls started to show once winning its wars became more challenging. Slowly but surely, Israel's existence came under threat, to the point that the war in 1967 was seen by many as a potential new Holocaust in which the Jewish people for the second time would run the risk of being exterminated completely. Although Israel was miraculously saved from destruction, the later wars proved to be extremely traumatic for world Jewry, and especially so for Israel's citizens.

With an increase in Arab hostility, terrorist attacks, more wars, more loss of life, many Israelis became convinced that the eternal condition of Jewish suffering could not be escaped. With the outbreak of the Intifada, with its continuous stream of suicide bombings, this feeling of hopelessness became even stronger. Simultaneously, Israel lost its credibility and admiration among large parts of the world community when it was forced to defend itself against the Palestinian populace, using last-resort tactics it had hoped to avoid. An outbreak of anti-Semitism in Europe came shortly after.

As if it were just waiting for an opportunity to turn its back on the Jews, Europe used Israel's self-defense as a provocation for anti-Semitic attacks on its own Jewish communities and on Israel. Comparing Israel's army to the Nazis, European countries accused Israel of stealing land from the Palestinians and managed to rewrite the history of the Middle East in radically anti-Semitic ways.

Israel as a Source of Anti-Semitism

The State of Israel, which was supposed to serve as a beacon for the Jewish people, suddenly seemed to be the source of its undoing. Jews had always been taught that the State of Israel was the solution to anti-Semitism, and now Israel was being used throughout Europe as the reason to justify anti-Semitic hatred. What was supposed to normalize the Jewish people, only increased the Jewish people's utter otherness. As such many Israelis became more and more convinced that the original Zionist program to rescue the Jewish people from this status as Other, failed miserably.

On a deeper level the ramifications were even more radical. The perceived failure of Zionism to bring about an end to anti-Semitism robbed many Israelis and Jews of their recently acquired sense of Jewish pride. Israel was seen as a source of shame. Once more Jews had to face their vulnerability. The international press made it virtually impossible to rely on the State of Israel to provide the foundation for a positive Jewish identity.

Neither the Holocaust nor the State of Israel yielded a meaningful definition of Jewishness. What the early Zionist leaders did not realize, or perhaps, did not want to realize, was that a State cannot create its own meaning. The State's role is to secure and make tangible a prior set of values and history that exist independent from the State. No political entity can provide the sole meaning in the lives of its citizens. States can at best, create the conditions under which a population can flourish. The State of Israel can do no more than to make sure that Jews are able to uphold their Jewishness, to increase their commitment to Jewish values, and if necessary, to defend our people against attack. To call upon the State to provide our Jewish identity, independent of the Judaism, is a naïve and self-destructive dream.

The "Signon" Problem

> "And it came to pass in the morning watch, that God looked down to the camp of the Egyptians through a pillar of fire and cloud and brought the camp of the Egyptians into confusion." (*Shemot* 14:24)

This verse, describing the moment when the Jews stood at the edge of the Red Sea with the Egyptian army in pursuit, is of great importance to us in our quest to uncover the deeper meaning and purpose of "identity." Rashi in his commentary is particularly taken here by the concept of confusion. In what way did God confuse the Egyptian camp?

"He befuddled them and took away their reason."[10] In other words, God denied the Egyptians the ability to use their faculty of reason, and that ultimately brought about their defeat. They were, seemingly, no longer able to think clearly. Their lack of mental clarity caused them to pursue the Jews into the parted sea, in spite of the clear signs that God Himself was guiding and protecting them. And so they drowned when the water came crashing down upon them.

---

[10] ad loc.

However, there is more to Rashi's observation than meets the eye.[11] In Hebrew Rashi uses the word "signon" which is conventionally translated as "reason," but this word implies much more than just logical thinking. To fully understand Rashi, we must turn to a most intriguing passage in the Talmud (Sanhedrin 89a), in which the rabbis try to offer a clear methodology for unmasking a false prophet. The legitimacy of a prophet, it turns out, depends on a special quality that the Talmud calls "signon", the same word used by Rashi: "One 'signon' is revealed to many prophets, yet no two prophets prophesize in an identical 'signon.'"

The conventional translation of "signon" in this case, is "communication" or "phraseology," but this translation fails to resonate with the Talmud's deeper intention. Again Rashi (in his commentary on this passage), comes to our aid, and simultaneously throws light on his earlier observation concerning the confusion of the Egyptian camp.

He explains that when God communicates with several prophets, He uses a single phraseology, and also expresses the message with one kind of "intonation." This is the meaning of "One signon is revealed to many prophets." In other words, God's style of communicating doesn't vary when He speaks to different prophets. God apparently has a very specific and personal way of doing things. When it comes to communicating with His prophets, God expresses His message in a form that is innate to Him and no other.

However, when prophets pass God's word on to the people of Israel, each one does this in his own way. Each one has his own signon. When conveying God's words, each prophet uses his own style and intonation since each prophet is essentially unique in his

---

[11] I am indebted to my *"mechutan"* and friend Rabbi Chaim Walkin, *"mashgiach ruchani"* at Ateret Yisrael Yeshiva, Jerusalem, for making me aware of this insight.

nature and psychological composition. This fact is essential to understanding prophecy: All prophecy is filtered through the personality of the prophet, and as such always carries an element of the prophet's distinctive individuality.[12] As such, the prophet as medium becomes part of his prophetic message, which ultimately enables him to convey God's word to the people in the most powerful and effective way. But since (and this is crucial to Rashi's argument), two prophets are necessarily two separate individuals, each one with his own style, it is impossible for them to use an identical phraseology or intonation. So that in the case they do, it is a clear indication that something is wrong and that one or both of them are false. One is imitating the other and therefore lacks authenticity.

This is the deeper meaning of Rashi's statement concerning the confusion of the Egyptians. The confusion which the Egyptians experienced at the time they pursued the Jews at the Red Sea was a severe identity crisis. God took away their sense of identity and purpose, and this became their undoing. The Egyptians no longer knew who they were. They got confused about their essence and lost their distinctive "signon."

As such they lost all direction even to the extent that they could no longer rationally deal with their earlier hatred for Jews. As Sartre predicts, their hatred for Jews increased because of this lack of authenticity.

---

[12] The only exception to this rule is Moshe who on certain occasions became the direct vehicle through which God spoke as if God was speaking Himself. See for example Rashi and many other commentaries on Devarim 30:1. See also Megilah 31a.

Man is Only Himself

In a most enlightening essay, the famous *Mashgiach* of the former Mir Yeshiva, Rabbi Yerucham Leibovits, discusses the importance of having a clear sense of identity:

> "Man is only himself, i.e., his inner life. And every move he makes against his inner essence, and especially when he focuses on his appearance (i.e., what kind of impression he likes to make) he becomes a stranger to himself and will deny his very self.
> Because man is able to move out of himself without end, and as such can lose himself completely, he will wander around without a place and without recognizable surroundings, and he will not be able to hold on to anything."[13]

This indeed is the greatest evil that can befall a man; the loss of his selfhood. One is reminded of Sartre's observation that we only become what we are by the radical and deep-seated refusal of that which others have made of us. The constant desire of most men to be something other than what they really are is one of the greatest tragedies of our times. To be authentically oneself in a world that strives night and day to mold us into something Other, is perhaps the greatest battle that man needs to fight if he wants to stay sane and significant. Once one has lost one's "signon" one has basically lost everything, because a man's signon is what makes him into an individual who he can recognize as himself – as a being that has no equivalent. A man's signon is the foundation of his self-awareness and self respect.

---

[13] Rabbi Yerucham Leibovits, *Da'at Chochma U-Mussar.*

Moshe's Identity Paradox

Surprisingly enough, it was Moshe Rabeinu who had to deal with the problem of signon-identity more than any other. When looking at his life, we are struck by the fact that it was he who became the greatest teacher of Israel. While we would have imagined that such a leader could only emerge from a strong Jewish background, the story of Moshe shows us otherwise. Moshe is brought up in a non-Jewish, or even anti-Jewish, environment after Pharaoh's daughter saves him from the river. Growing up in Pharaoh's house, he was utterly disconnected from his people, hardly aware that he was a Jew. Years later, as a grown man, he encountered his true self, which led to one of the most heroic moments in Jewish history.

While still part of Pharaoh's household, Moshe suddenly decides to go see his brothers, the Jews. This confrontation with Self proves to be perhaps the most crucial moment in all of his life.

> "And it came to pass in these days that Moshe grew up and went out to his brothers. And he saw their burden and he saw an Egyptian striking a Hebrew, one of his brothers. And he looked left and right and he saw that there was no man, and he struck the Egyptian and buried him in the sand." (*Shemot* 11:2).

This whole episode is concealed in mystery. What made Moshe suddenly decide to go and see his brothers? How did he know that these were "his brothers" in the first place? What caused him to take the side of the Hebrew instead of the Egyptian? What is the significance of first "looking left and right," and only than striking the Egyptian?

Moshe, once grown up, somehow felt that he was different from the other men in Pharaoh's house. Something deep within him must have told him that the slaves living at the other side of the fence were related to him, and he was compelled to have a look. This led to an encounter with something he could not have anticipated: anti-Semitism and his own authenticity! Once he saw the Egyptian officer strike the Jew, Moshe experienced a most intricate dilemma. On whose side was he going to be? It would have been entirely natural for him to take the side of the Egyptian. The Egyptian belonged to the culture with which he was familiar. This was his world, and he certainly must have heard a lot about "those Jews" who refused to adopt the Egyptians' ways. These were a people who had their own religion and a culture removed entirely from the world of Egyptian polytheism; and this created a strong feeling of hatred amongst Egyptians for their Jewish slaves.

For Moshe, this must have been a moment of profound identity crisis. Where do I belong? Who am I? For a moment Moshe does not know what to do.

And he Looked Left and Right

Suddenly these words: "And he looked left and right" take on a much deeper significance. He looked one way and he saw the world of Egypt, then he looked the other way and saw the world of the Israelites. And he realized that there was no man, i.e., that he himself could not claim to be a man as long as he remained caught between two worlds. It is utterly impossible to be a man in this world unless one has a clear identity. In that split second Moshe decides. "And he struck the Egyptian and buried him in the sand." In a moment of violence and total clarity, Moshe resolves his identity crisis and buries the Egyptian within himself, determining once and for all that his lot should be with the Israelites.[14]

---

[14] This unique interpretation was orally transmitted to me. The "author" is unknown.

Moshe's choice created a revolution in his own life, and radically transformed the whole of Jewish history. In a split second, Moshe found his signon, and only then was able to start his real life. It is from that moment onwards that the greatest revolutionary movement in all human history starts to take place. Moshe's becoming an authentic Jew heralds all the other great revolutions that continue to shape world history. It was the moment that led to the foundation of mankind's liberty, and through which it became possible for God's ethical message for humanity to become part of our physical reality. Once man becomes aware of his identity and accepts his mission as a free moral being, then his real story begins.

Speech Impediment

However, identity formation does not usually happen overnight. It is a process that requires great effort and struggle. To give birth to identity is to experience moments of utter despair and also great victory. But the most crucial moment is the moment when man makes up his mind to discover his identity, and own his life. This matter is bared out in an episode that follows from Moshe's authentic Jewish awakening. Still far from sure yet what his identity is really all about, Moshe meets God at the burning bush. Here God commands him to return to Egypt to challenge Pharaoh and to liberate his people. Moshe is overwhelmed and shocked by this divine demand. Nothing is further from his mind than to lead this people, with whom he never had any real connection, to freedom. As a result a most surprising and unprecedented dispute between man and God takes place.

> "And God said, 'I have seen the suffering of my people...and I have heard their cries…and I have come down to save them from

> the clutches of the Egyptians…and take them up…to the land flowing with milk and honey…
> "So now come, that I may send you to Pharaoh and take My people, the children of Israel, out of Egypt.' Moshe said to God, 'Who am I that I should go to Pharaoh and that I should take the children of Israel out of Egypt?' (God) replied, 'for I will be with you and this is the sign that I have sent you.'
> "Also when you take the people out of Egypt you (all) will serve God on this mountain.' Moshe said to God, 'When I will be coming to the children of Israel and say to them, 'The God of your forefathers has sent me to you,' they will ask, 'What is His name?' ' What shall I answer them?' God said to Moshe (to tell them) 'I am whomever I am…'"
> "Moshe said to God, 'Please, O Lord I am not a man of words – not yesterday, not the day before… for I stammer and have difficulty speaking.'" *(Shemot* 3:7–4:10).

Moshe's objections are most intriguing. How can he argue with the Creator of the Universe? Although this divine encounter must have come to him as a complete surprise, it is not that fact per se, that he cannot accept. What seems to bother him is that he himself is not able to speak well, and definitely not to Pharaoh! Moshe claims that he is not a "man of words," yet nearly everything else we know about Moshe's life demonstrates his unusual talent for public speaking (e.g., nearly the whole book of *Devarim* is a single lengthy speech he gave before he died!). We clearly need to investigate the deeper meaning of this supposed inability to speak.

It is possible that Moshe's refusal to speak was not born out of a physical speech impediment, but rather from his lack of a clear identity from which he could form a coherent position. Just because a person recognizes that he is a Jew doesn't mean that he understands the content of his identity. And such was Moshe's situation, so that he doubted his ability to effectively complete the mission that God gave him. How can I stand in front of Pharaoh and argue that he should let the Israelites go, if I do not yet fully realize what an Israelite is? No doubt Pharaoh will realize that I am not really, fully one of them. I may belong to their tribe but I have not yet become one of them in spirit, and this will make my argument weak. My authenticity is not yet well established! A man cannot fight for something unless he knows what it is he's fighting for! After all, it is not the physical liberty of the Jews that You, God, most desire. Primarily what You want is to liberate the Israelites spiritually, and so how can I confront Pharaoh when it is not clear to me what that means?

But Who Are You?

Then, suddenly, in the middle of the debate, Moshe turns the argument around. Instead of responding to God's questions, he asks God a question – one that may very well be seen as the ultimate chutzpah. You want me to tell the Israelites that the God of their fathers has sent me to them, but they will ask me, "What is His name?"

What difference would it make whether Moshe knows God's name or not? If he tells the elders of Israel that God appointed him to lead the people out of slavery, does he really think they won't be interested in what he has to say because he does not know God's official name? On a deeper level, this projected question of the Israelites is in fact Moshe's own question, and at the heart of the issue is a question of a most profound nature.

I do not know who I am, but even so, tell me who You are? What is Your identity? When we read this question for the first time, we get the impression that Moshe does not know to Whom he is speaking.

Since when is man able to ask God about His identity? Is it not extremely arrogant to think that God has to explain himself to man? Nevertheless, God understands Moshe's inquiry. By asking who God is, Moshe is really looking for a way to fully understand his own identity. Only when we understand our source, can we understand our selves. The Jew especially, is defined by the special relationship he has with his Creator. If I am essentially, part of a relationship with God, then only when I understand this relationship and the being to Whom I am relating, do I really attain self-knowledge as a Jew. Only when man acknowledges and experiences in the core of his being that he is created in God's image, can he know who he is. But that means that he must have some idea of what that Image is all about. Only then does self-knowledge become possible.

Therefore, it is only Moshe's consciousness of God that enables him to understand his mission. Only consciousness of his Creator can give him the strength to confront Pharaoh and fulfill God's commandment!

In fact, since everything else in this world is affected by external forces, and is subject to change, the only stable source of identity is God. God's identity is by definition absolute. God's response now resonates to us in a beautifully simple and harmonic way: "I am who ever I am." The secret to identity is authenticity. Nothing from without which is not part of My essence affects My being. I will surely influence outer forces but they will not change My essence. In fact it is My essence that gives Me the power to affect the world around Me. And so you, Moshe, must try to develop a similar attitude. Once you have tapped the root of your inner self, which is so inherently connected with My image, you will be able to achieve full authenticity, and then the faculty of speech will be yours. When you are no longer swayed by external forces, your deepest essential being will reveal itself.

Gentile Reminders

Jewish continuity and survival depends upon Jews recognizing that their identities spring from thousands of years of carrying out a divine mission. Neither the Holocaust nor the State of Israel will provide them with a solid identity. If we want to survive, and if we believe that it matters whether or not there are Jews in the world, then we must look back into our traditions, re-evaluate them, and come to understand ourselves as essentially Jewish Selves.

In a world in which Jews have lost their sense of Jewishness, it seems that God sometimes comes to remind them of who they are through the wise words of the gentiles. Sometimes it is *they* who recognize the Jews as the instrument through which God's divine plan for the world is to be realized.

The Russian novelist Leo Tolstoy wrote the following words:

> "The Jew is that sacred being who has brought down from heaven the everlasting fire, and has illumined with it the entire world. He is the religious source, spring and fountain out of which all the rest of the peoples have drawn their beliefs and their religions."[15]

In our days it was Thomas Cahill who in his own admirable way wrote:

> "The Jews gave us the Outside and the Inside – our outlook and our inner life. We can hardly get up in the morning or cross the Street without being Jewish. We dream Jewish dreams and hope Jewish hopes. Most of our best words, in fact – new, adventure, surprise, unique, individual, person, vocation, time, history, future,

---

[15] Quoted by Chief Rabbi J. H. Hertz, *A Book of Jewish Thought*, London, Oxford University Press, 1966, p.135.

freedom, progress, spirit, faith, hope, justice – are the gifts of the Jews."[16]

This indeed is the real identity of the Jew. Over vast regions of space and time, he has carried the words of God, and by that he became the natural representative of this Word, influencing his fellow men in every generation. Once he rediscovers this mission, he will rediscover his identity; and then his problems, and those of the world, will be resolved. Because it is only through the word of God that man can hope to find his redemption.

---

[16] Thomas Cahill, *The Gifts of the Jews*, Double Day, NY, 1998.p.240–241.

Chapter 5

WHY THE *KASHRUT* LAWS WERE GIVEN SO LATE

NOTHING BRINGS TO LIGHT more about a book than it's beginning, the Torah being no exception. As such, the opening remarks of Rashi to his Biblical commentary should prove most instructive. Asks Rashi, "Why does the Torah start with a narrative of the creation? If the Torah is meant to be a guide for how to live the best possible life, why not skip rather to the first law delivered to the Jewish people as a whole?" "And this month shall be the first of months..." (*Shemot* 12:2). With this simple question, Rashi opens up a Pandora's box of other queries about the Torah's intent. Is it an historical narrative, relaying to us the moral message of our ancestors' successes and failures? Or is it rather a codex of law, coming to teach us precisely which acts evoke God's blessings and which provoke His ire? No sooner do we focus on one of these aspects than we are confronted by the other. So here lies the problem: one cannot neatly divide the Torah between its didactic and legalistic elements. True, the first book and a half of the five Books of Moses consist mainly of narrative, but from that point on the program switches back and forth, creating a dynamic interchange of law and lore.

The Earlier and the Later

Whenever we attempt to figure out why any given portion appears precisely in the place that it does, we find ourselves most perplexed. Is this the correct location for this law or story? Would it not have made more sense elsewhere? How does it relate within this particular context? Since the author of the book is none other than the Creator of the Universe, who designed the human body and set the planets in their orbits, and who is perfect and omniscient, it follows that each word and letter of His manifesto should fit into a logical, organic pattern.

Questions regarding the organizational structure of the Torah have become the stock-in-trade of Biblical commentary. It is not uncommon to find the greatest of our commentators asking how a certain section relates to that which came before it or why this or that particular law seems to have been written out of place. All in all, no one seems quite content with the order of the Torah as we have it before us. And rightly so, because no matter how you slice it, the Torah at first glance does not seem to follow the type of logical progression that we would expect from the greatest book of all time.

As if there were not yet enough confusion, the proposed answers to these difficulties, rather than providing any consensus, actually branch off into many far-ranging philosophical disputes. We even find arguments on such a fundamental issue as to whether the Torah is bound to a chronological pattern at all. Some maintain the view that *ein mukdam o'muchar baTorah* – that there is no *before* or *after* in the Torah. But even according to them, this rule may sometimes be circumvented. But if the Torah may depart from an historical sequence, when exactly will it conform to the rule of order and when not? What meta-principles dictate the deviations from the natural time-line?

Before attempting to answer these questions, I would like to propose yet another. While it may seem innocuous enough at first, once pondered it will open up new and daring vistas of thought. If we correctly reflect upon its meaning, as indeed we must do, we will be drawn to make some provocative conclusions as to the purpose of the *mitzvot* and the nature of man.

Tip of the Iceberg

The question, originally put forward by the renowned Italian scholar Rabbi Ovadia Seforno (1470–1550), is concerned specifically with *kashrut*, Jewish dietary law, and also with *taharat hamishpacha*, Jewish family purity laws. These laws seem to arrive too late in the Biblical narrative, appearing for the first time in the book of *Vayikra*, the third of the five books of the Torah. Why in fact do these *mitzvot*, so essential to Jewish living, not find their place earlier in the text? We would probably expect their introduction in the book of *Shemot*, along with so many other basic tenets of Judaism. There we find the Ten Commandments as well as the *mishpatim*, which together form the basis of Jewish civil law. But where are the laws of *kashrut*? Where are the laws of family purity? The Torah almost treats them as afterthoughts. Or perhaps even worse. Perhaps the late-game introduction of these laws intimates to us that they are problematic.

But that is really only the tip of the iceberg. Once we start asking questions like these, we can go on and on. Let us ask yet another: why was the Torah itself given so late in history? Jews had been around for hundreds of years before the revelation at Mount Sinai. Why didn't God present the Torah to the first Jews, Avraham, Yitzchak, and Ya'akov? True, the forefathers kept many of the *mitzvot*, but they did so only on a voluntary basis, as a result of their own derivations about the spiritual reality, and not because they had been commanded to do so by God. Only much later in Jewish history do we find *mitzvot* actually coming to us by way of divine decree. One might logically infer that the earlier generations simply did not need the Torah. But if the Torah is the eternal Truth – the blueprint of creation – then surely its statutes must have universal relevance? What is the Torah if its message has temporal limitations?

Breaking Point

The discussion of the Torah's chronological sequencing revolves around a singular event in Jewish history. As such, this pivotal event must be our point of departure for the journey into the world that Rabbi Ovadia Seforno wants us to enter. The episode to which I refer is the *Chet ha'Egel*, the Sin of the Golden Calf.

A mere forty days after the Creator of the universe revealed Himself with the words, "I am the Lord, your God," the Jewish people sank into sinful idolatry. Moshe had ascended above to receive the Tablets of the Covenant, but he tarried too long for the eager masses waiting at mountain's foot. After forty days and forty nights, many assumed that Moshe simply ceased to exist as a physical being and would not be returning to them. In their desperation the people turned to Moshe's brother, Aharon, asking him to build them an idol to compensate for the loss of their leader. As a golden calf emerged from the dazzling fire, those taken in by its charm declared, "These are your gods, O Israel." The shocking contrast of this spiritual nadir to the exalted heights they experienced just forty days before could not be any starker.

As difficult as it is to make sense of the Sin of the Golden Calf (and we will explore its significance), what proves even more difficult to understand is the debate over when it took place. As noted, in the historical progression of events, it took place exactly forty days after the Jewish people received the Torah. The question though, lies within the text itself; Is the story of the Golden Calf ordered sequentially with regard to the other events recorded before and after it, or not?

This question takes on special significance in relation to God's command to build the *Mishkan*, the Tent of Meeting that served as a prototype for what would later be the Temple. Was that command issued before the *Chet ha'Egel*, as we find clearly indicated in the text of the Torah before us, or is the Torah's presentation of these events entirely out of order. Did the institution of the *Mishkan* actually come after the sin? While this line of inquiry may sound academic, the consequences of its resolution ripple through the entire foundation of Jewish thought.

The Dispute

The attempts to place the command to build the *Mishkan* in a timeline vis-a-vis the *Chet ha'Egel* are a source of major dispute among the classical commentators. The Ramban holds that the command took place long before the sin – that it was actually decreed shortly after the revelation at Sinai. After forging a covenant with God and agreeing to be His treasured nation, it was only fitting for the Jews to have a place where God could rest His presence amongst them. From this haven God would speak with Moshe and issue forth *mitzvot* for the Jewish people. We see, therefore, that according to the Ramban, the *Mishkan* held an intrinsically necessary function, always critical to Jewish belief and praxis.[1]

Rashi, however, takes an altogether different approach. We find that the Torah refers to the *Mishkan* as "*Mishkan ha'edut*," a sanctuary of testimony. To what did the *Mishkan* testify, asks Rashi? To the fact that God had forgiven us for the Golden Calf (*Shemot* 38:21). After threatening to destroy the Jewish people for worshipping it, the very command to build the *Mishkan* gave testimony to the fact that God desired to draw close to us once again.

Against the Ramban's protests, we hear Rashi's opinion clearly stating that the *Mishkan* came into conception only *after* the *Chet ha'Egel*. Had the Jewish people not built the Golden Calf, we never would have needed a *Mishkan*.

[1] Ramban, Introduction to *Shemot*.

A New World Order

Rabbi Ovadia Seforno follows Rashi's line but takes him one step further. In a way, with Seforno we arrive at the logical conclusion of Rashi's hypothesis – that the institution of the *Mishkan* represented a much more fundamental transformation.

The Torah introduces the command to build the *Mishkan* with the following words: "Make Me a sanctuary that I may dwell among you. Just as I have shown you, the structure of the *Mishkan* and the structure of its vessels, so shall you do." (*Shemot* 25:8–9)

Here, Seforno makes a most fascinating comment:

> "...so shall you do in order that I [God] may dwell among you [Israel], speaking with you and accepting your prayers and the service. But not as the matter stood before the *Chet ha'Egel*, as it had been said previously, In any place...I will come to you" (*Shemot* 20:24).

After the sin, we only have one place to seek God: the *Mishkan*. But it had not always been that way. Earlier in our history, we could seek God in any place, and He in turn would come to us. Not only did we not need the *Mishkan*, but neither would we have needed the Temple in Jerusalem. Even Jerusalem itself would never have risen to any special significance. Were it not for the Sin of the Golden Calf, the whole world would have been a Temple, the entire universe a Jerusalem. Since God is everywhere, we really should be able to serve Him anywhere.

One can easily see that Judaism wore a much different face before the advent of the *Chet ha'Egel*. The religion was essentially decentralized, and perhaps even more open and free-spirited. One needed no pilgrimage to a holy site. Every home was a temple and every corner a possible place of worship. And what is perhaps most astounding of all, is that this is the way it would have remained! Were it not for the sin of the *Egel*, we never would have acquired any limitations on our service of God.

But the situation changes drastically after the *Chet ha'Egel*. God, to be sure, is still everywhere, but our service now requires constraints, becoming bound within an all-too-specific realm. The *Mishkan* can offer us a symbol of God's omnipresence, drawing our awareness toward that lofty realization, but we no longer have the freedom to act as if we really live on the plane of that elevated consciousness. From now on we may serve God only in the precise place and in the meticulous manner in which He instructs us. Hence our need for a *Mishkan*, a Temple, and a Holy City.

Holding on to Time

Reflecting back on all that has been said, one cannot help but wonder why the Sin of the Golden Calf should have necessitated such a radical alteration in the method of our divine worship? Where exactly did we go wrong?

The first point to explore must be the sin itself, because, at least at face value, it really appears to make no sense at all. How could a people who had just witnessed a divine revelation turn around such a short time later and serve an idol? They heard the word of God telling them, "Do not make a graven image." How could they have doubted that their machinations would meet with anything other than the Creator's full wrath? Nevertheless, our people sinned, falling from the heights of revelation to the depths of idolatry within the span of a mere forty days.

So implausible and paradoxical is this event, that a surface-level understanding simply cannot hold water. The experience of revelation was too awe-inspiring, too overpowering for such a turnabout to be comprehensible without deeper analysis.

Only when we see the "meta-physics" beneath the story of the Golden Calf, do we get an understanding of how the Jewish people could behave in such a seemingly fickle manner. And in fact, it turns out that the two events – the revelation and the idolatry – rather than contradicting one another, are actually entirely complementary, like a particle and a wave. On a deeper level of reality, the *Chet ha'Egel* issues forth as the direct and logical consequence of the Sinai experience. Built in to that very experience came a need, a desire to build the *Egel.* As absurd as it sounds, the revelation of God actually led in a rational causal progression to the sin.

How does this work? The answer is actually rather simple: it is one thing to experience direct spiritual revelation; and it is quite another to hold on to it. Spirituality is not difficult to experience, especially when one is confronted from the outside by the Deity. Anyone can receive revelation if God chooses to oblige. The challenge lies in maintaining that degree of inspiration once the moment of encounter has passed. Inspiration comes in a momentary high but living the rest of one's life with the awareness once granted in a fleeting moment, often proves to be an exponentially more difficult challenge. Passing that inspiration on to the next generation is of course, even more onerous. The revelation certainly made an impression, but like all experiences, Sinai too fades from consciousness with the passing of time. How then to preserve the effect of the greatest event in all of human history? To let it slide would have been a tragedy of the highest order. The Jews at Sinai understood this problem, and therefore came up with a plan. They knew that the nature of experience is ephemeral, so they devised a way to hold on to Sinai permanently, both for themselves and for all future generations. Their solution was what we call the Golden Calf.

Symbolic Sinai

In reality, the Jews did with the Golden Calf what we all do whenever forced to grapple with an abstract concept: we make a model. When the true grasp of an idea evades us, we seek tangible substitutes for the intangible. That is why it is not uncommon to find scientists utilizing models to understand the most intangible elements of our world, such as the structure of the atom or the curvature of space-time. Likewise, this explains why the Rabbis of the Talmud always discussed concrete legal cases or taught philosophical ideas by way of metaphor. We humans need models to perceive abstract concepts.

We all experience moments of breakthrough. At these times, as when lightning flashes in the pitch of darkness, we are shown a brief glimpse of the hidden. But the impact of such experiences, as we have noted, is all too fleeting. Therefore, if we wish to recreate the inspiration, we will need to have something to remind us of it. A model provides just such a tool. It helps us to tap into the lofty awareness we once grasped in totality but that has now dissipated into a mist of ambiguity. A model serves as a medium to transform the esoteric and metaphysical into more user-friendly, human, terms. As such, it provides the key for concretizing the transitory impressions left by our transcendent experiences.

The Jews felt that they could never live in the higher world, relating so abstractly to the absolute awareness of God's existence. As such, they sought to translate their experience of revelation into more tangible, palatable, and transmittable terms. The alternative, they thought, would have meant losing the experience forever. After a while even they might have fallen into disbelief about whether or not the revelation had actually taken place; and how much more so later generations. Therefore, in an attempt to capture what they experienced for posterity and to eliminate the potential for doubt, the Jews fashioned the ultimate memento.

The *Egel* Uncovered

It may prove difficult for us today to appreciate why a statue of a baby cow would be the most effective symbol for the most sublime experience in human history. The Golden Calf does not seem to us to capture the essence of Divine revelation. However, this lack of understanding comes from our crude translation of the Torah's term "*Egel hazahav.*" Translating this phrase as "golden calf" cheapens its meaning immeasurably. We must look deeper into its symbolism to truly understand what the *Egel hazahav* was really all about.

To the Jews at Sinai, the *Egel* represented a metaphysical reality – an abstract demonstration of God's dominion over creation. In fact, we find that when the prophets experienced the height of divine inspiration, the *Egel* was always part of their vision. The revelation recorded in the prophecy of Yechezkel, known as the *Ma'a'se Merkava* (the Act of the Chariot), relates the deepest of kabalistic secrets about the relationship of the Creator to his creation. Not surprisingly, the *Egel* plays a prominent role in that vision, described as one of the four images engraved on God's "chariot." While a full analysis of this topic is beyond the scope of these pages, we must nevertheless appreciate that whatever its ultimate meaning, the *Egel* is certainly neither simple nor merely absurd.

Hence we come to relate to the *Egel hazahav* in a completely new light. Much more than a mere idol, it was a symbol representing a metaphysical reality in the upper worlds. As a model, it served to invoke the spirit of revelation to all those who viewed it. Hence, the *Egel* became a realistic and pragmatic attempt to capture the Sinai experience. It was a tool for the preservation of revelation.

The Distinction

While all this helps to explain how the Jewish people could have come to build the Golden Calf, what now escapes our understanding is why it was viewed as such a sin. God protests the building of the calf in the strongest terms, threatening to destroy the Jews and to create a new people out of Moshe's progeny in their place. But in light of what we now know to be the intent behind the *Egel*, what was actually so wrong about building it?

What makes this even more difficult to understand is the fact that inside the *Mishkan*, which God Himself commanded us to build, we find another *Egel* of sorts. The only difference between the Egel and the symbol employed in the *Mishkan* is that this time the graven image takes the form of two children rather than a calf. The *keruvim* (cherubs) were also golden statues, yet God actually commands us to place them right inside the *Mishkan* – in the Holy of the Holies no less! Moreover, it was from the space between the two *keruvim* that God communicated directly with Moshe. The *keruvim* stood as guards at the portal between the physical and the spiritual worlds. There is nothing more holy on Earth. And yet, like the *Egel*, they too were just statues. They too were just symbols. Hence we are left wondering why the *Egel* that the Jews created on their own accord was so much worse than the *keruvim* that God commanded them to make.

The answer, of course, is just that: one was initiated by man and the other by God. When man makes an *Egel*, it is a sin of the highest magnitude; But when God makes one, He creates holiness in space. The distinction is anything but arbitrary. When man, in his limited understanding and insufficient imagination, attempts to create a representation of the transcendent revelation experience, he is destined to fail. The ability to craft the appropriate symbol lies beyond his limited capacity. And when a symbol lacks accuracy of representation, it fails completely as an appropriate symbol. And then the object becomes at best a cartoonish caricature, and at worst an idol. However, God, who completely comprehends the object of representation, knows how to fashion its symbol correctly. Only God can conceive of a symbol that captures the true essence of holiness.

Intent vs. Content

The explanation of the sin of the Golden Calf outlined above was originally put forward by the medieval Spanish philosopher and poet, Rabbi Yehuda HaLevi, in his magnum opus, *The Kuzari.* True to its author's artistic spirit, *The Kuzari* presents an apologetic for the Jewish faith by way of a hypothetical conversation between two unlikely protagonists: a righteous non-Jewish king of the Khazar people and his friend, a Jewish sage.

The king had always been a very pious man in his own right, a man devoted single-mindedly to the service of God as he understood it within the framework of his native religion. But his curiosity about other faiths is piqued by a certain dream, oft repeated in his night time slumber, in which he is told, "Your intention is pleasing to the Creator, but not your manner of acting."[2]

This vision sends the king on a search for truth that engages him with thinking men of different faiths – Greek philosophy, Christianity, and Islam. Eventually his search for the true path brings him into contact with a learned Rabbi. During the course of their discussion, the sage leads the king through a tour de force of Jewish philosophy, ultimately convincing the king of Judaism's veracity. The king then converts to the faith of the Jews, along with his entire kingdom.

At the point where their conversation focuses on the *Chet ha'Egel*, the sage explains to the king the secret behind this sin. The problem, he tells him, arose in that the building of the *Egel* had not issued forth as a mandate by God. The people sinned by putting their own initiative before God's expressed wishes.

[2] *The Kuzari*, 1.1.

To his credit, the astute king understands the implications of what the sage tells him. At this point he bursts forth in a sudden epiphany that captures the crux of the issue precisely:

Behold, you have confirmed for me the opinion that I arrived at through meditation as well as that which I saw in my dream, and that is: the only way by which man may hope to reach the sublime is to be directed to it by the Sublime, through actions dictated by God. (1:98)

Like the Khazar king, the Jewish people failed in their actions to reach the divine despite their virtuous intentions. Man does not enjoy the freedom of choosing his own path to God. He must rather be guided upon that road by none other than God Himself.

The Jewish people meant well, but that did not suffice. Building the *Egel* on their own accord was wrong, no matter how noble the cause. The principle we learn from their mistake is that the noble intentions that motivate an action do not make it righteous. Only the divinely willed content of an action can give it real positive moral value.

Divine Concession

In place of the *Egel*, God gives us the *Mishkan* – the true symbol of that which we sought to represent with the *Egel*. But He agrees to this compromise with a sense of regret, as it were. Service via *Mishkan* is not God's ideal manner of worship, but with the *Chet ha'Egel*, man proved himself incapable of relating to God in purely abstract, non-symbolic terms. Man demonstrated his weakness, admitting that he cannot live on an entirely elevated plane, constantly aware of God's presence. It has proven too difficult for him to realize that the entire universe is a single Temple. Ultimate reality must be watered down for him and translated into his own terms; he can only relate to it through the medium of a tangible symbol.

With the *Egel* we mistakenly attempted to make our own symbolic representation. God therefore supplies us with the real one, namely the *Mishkan*. As conceived by Rashi and Seforno, then, the *Mishkan* represents a divine concession to man's spiritual weakness.

Listen to Rashi's translation of "*Mishkan ha'edut*," the dwelling place of testimony:

> "*Edut l'Yirael* she'viter *la'hem HaKadosh Baruch Hu al ma'a'se he'Egel.* It is testimony to Israel that God *conceded* to them regarding the incident of the Calf" (*Shemot* 38:21).

With the *Egel* we showed that we needed to translate the revelation experience into our own terms. Henceforth, with the *Mishkan*, God provides us with just that. He gives us a specific and unique place to worship, a place where it will be all the more possible to recreate the inspiration of Sinai, a place where we can palpably experience the presence of God. But as inspirational as that sounds, and as magnificent as it must have been, the Holy One never intended it as anything more than a compromise. In the realm of the ideal, the cosmos serve as God's *Mishkan*.

A Healthy Diet

Taking this insight into account, we can now begin to understand Seforno's answer to our original enquiry: why were the *kashrut* and purity laws introduced so late? Why, after all, do we only learn about them after the *Chet ha'Egel*, and not before? The answer, as we shall see, relates precisely to the incident of the Golden Calf.

> And God spoke to Moshe and to Aharon saying to them: Speak to the Children of Israel saying, "This is the type of animal that you may eat..." (*Vayikra* 11:1–2).

With this verse the Torah presents us for the first time with the Jewish dietary laws – which animals we may eat and which we may not. At this point, Seforno delivers his own introduction to these laws:

> After the moment when Israel fell from the spiritual heights they had acquired at Sinai, a level upon which they were fitting for God to place His presence upon them without any medium or symbol...it became despicable to God to dwell amongst them at all. Until, that is, Moshe was able to achieve a degree of amelioration with his prayers, to the effect that now God would place His presence amongst them through the medium of the *Mishkan*...And so too, God saw fit to remedy their temperament so that it would be fitting for the light of eternal life, and this He accomplished through the regulation of diet and sexual relations (*ad loc*).

A most daring and remarkable thesis indeed! Just as the *Mishkan* had come as a concession to man's degraded spiritual status after the *Chet ha'Egel*, so too the laws of *kashrut* and family purity! In the same way that we lost the immediate impression of God's omnipresence, so too our entire ability to receive the influence of spirituality underwent a drastic transformation.

Before the *Chet ha'Egel*, the Jewish soul achieved such a rarefied degree of perfection that it became insusceptible to the influence of impurity, whether dietary or sexual. These things simply held no sway over our being. But now, in this lower level of existence, the influence of impurity threatens to dilute our spiritual sensitivities.

To put it bluntly, the basic message Seforno wishes to impart is this: when we are healthy we do not need a diet; nor do we need to regulate our sexual activity quite so much. But when we fall ill, our defenses are down and we become susceptible to detrimental influences upon our health. It is then that we need to follow a stricter diet and to watch our bodily activity with greater care.

Perhaps, one may ask, why should such mundane activity affect the state of our lofty souls? But to pose such a question would be to ignore the reality of our spiritual station after the Sin of the Golden Calf. Things have changed. The soul has now become susceptible to physical impurity. And hence, it must be treated appropriately. That is why God offers us an elixir in the form of dietary and sexual regulations.

But these *mitzvot* do more than just help us to ward off any further decline. To be sure, the reality of our spiritual standing after the *Chet ha'Egel* means that we have become susceptible to impurity. But what these laws actually accomplish is to raise us beyond the limitations of our condition, to bring us back to the exalted level that we occupied before the Sin of the Golden Calf.

The Timely Torah

Following this logic will help to answer the other question that we raised. Why didn't the original Jews, our holy forefathers, receive the Torah? Why was it left only to the later generations of their descendants?

The answer by now should appear quite obvious: the earlier generations simply did not need it. In their superior state of spiritual health they could serve God without the *mitzvot*. As such, they lived on a level higher even than that of the Jews at Sinai. And while they certainly kept many of the *mitzvot*, they did so not out of duty but as a natural expression of their closeness with God. Their service was a voluntary one issuing forth from the purity of their hearts without the need of Divine decree. They used the *mitzvot* to approach God, to come closer to Him, but they did not need them to combat a weak nature.

We need not rely on a mere extrapolation from the laws of *kashrut* for indeed we find that this insight permeated Seforno's entire interpretation of Biblical events. An example from his writings on the book of *Bereshit* should prove instructive:

The *parasha* of *Vayetze* records the births of the children born to Ya'akov, twelve sons from four wives. As the competition to produce the *shevatim* (the tribes of Israel) ensues, we are awe-struck by the devotion of our matriarchs in their desire to forge the nascent nation. As Rachel so eloquently states in her naming of Naftali, she had to resort to "sacred schemes" in order to ensure her portion of the Jewish heritage.

One problem that emerges from the story, however, is that it all takes place far too quickly. Even if there was some overlap in the pregnancies of Ya'akov's four wives (as Seforno suggests), at best we end up with nine births within seven years! In order to make this scenario at all practicable we are forced to make a crucial assumption: that each conception took place immediately after the birth of the previous child.

But what has happened to the laws of family purity? These laws provide for a period of restraint after the birth of a child. Leah, though, becomes pregnant over and over again far too quickly to allow for the observance of these laws. Therefore, concludes Seforno, it is possible that our forefathers simply did not keep the laws of family purity.

Seforno and Historicizing the *Mitzvot*

Our forefathers did not observe many of the laws we find in the Torah. We must realize of course, that this seeming lack of religiosity on their part is actually an expression of their incredible spiritual levels. They simply were unaffected by certain elements of impurity that held sway over their lesser descendants. Only in later generations did the Jews come to need more laws to counter the flaws in their nature. Our forefathers, though, still gigantic in their spiritual stature, simply did not require all the *mitzvot* to serve God correctly. They could be entirely religious, even without so much religion.

This insight has dangerous implications. It seems to suggest that the binding nature of the *mitzvot* changes with the times. One might wish to conclude that if there was once a time when certain *mitzvot* were not mandatory, then perhaps such a time may well come again? Or perhaps it has already come?

Of course, Seforno had no intention of historicizing the *mitzvot* (i.e., of weakening them by limiting their relevance within a particular historical context). Just the opposite! To understand Seforno properly is to realize that our relationship to the *mitzvot* only strengthens with time. From his perspective, the argument for historicization runs straight in the opposite direction. Times certainly change, but only for the worse. As history progresses, we require more intense devotion to the Torah and *mitzvot* in order to relate properly to God.

Progressive Regression

We usually think of progress in terms of scientific and technological advancement. Within such a framework, I admit, we may accurately describe the course of human development as a linear progression. As time marches on, our storehouse of knowledge grows exponentially, and so too our technical capabilities. However, seen in such a light, the present takes primacy while the past finds itself relegated to "the trash heap of history." Man could never have been more advanced than he is at this very moment.

From such a perspective, though, the words of King Solomon cry out emotively: "The superiority of man over beast is for naught"

(*Kohelet* 3:19). It would seem as if the difference was one of mere quantity of knowledge, not quality of being. But the Torah maintains a very different calculus for evaluating man's worth. Unlike the popular notion of progress as set within scientific parameters, Judaism measures human development with the yardstick of the soul. And unlike science, by this standard our talents have only waned with the passing of time.

This idea is known in Judaism as the doctrine of *yeridot hadorot*, the declination of the generations: each generation falls lower in spiritual status than the generation that preceded it. The qualities of the soul, such as moral fortitude and spiritual purity, only become diluted as the generations pass. As we grow increasingly aware of our physical drives and desires, our sensitivity to ethical issues and matters of the soul becomes all the more obscure. We may progress in our technological aptitude, inventing new machines and better cures, but this kind of extrinsic advancement fails to portray an accurate picture of our intrinsic development as human beings. As the unification of a body and a soul, man's progress can only be measured by the degree to which his spirit holds sway over his physical nature.

Man is much more than a maker of machines. What truly determines his worth is the degree of his moral perfection and closeness to God. As such, morality, purity, and spirituality provide the only genuine barometer of man's development. And by these criteria history records our degeneration.

A Modicum of Restraint

Seforno's extremely original approach applies the doctrine of *yeridot hadorot* to a global understanding of the *mitzvot*, with all that this implies. If previous generations stood on higher ground, then we can assume that their souls operated with less need for the *mitzvot*.

Conversely, as we fall farther with the passing of time, we become more in need of the *mitzvot.*

It must be must stressed, however, that this is a highly daring assumption, especially for such a relatively recent Torah commentator as Seforno. It would all rest much easier if we could find some backing for this thesis in the words of an earlier, perhaps even more classical, text of Jewish thought.

Such support can indeed be found in one of the classic works of Jewish philosophy entitled *Hovot haLevavot, Duties of the Heart* (Spain, 1040). Written by Rabbi Bachaya ibn Pakuda, this powerful treatise provides both a fundamental introduction to Jewish thought and comprehensive guide to character development. It is within these hallowed pages that we find a statement resonating with Seforno's wisdom.

Towards the end of the work, *Hovot haLevavot* discusses the character trait of restraint. Defining the term very generally as "a bridling of the inner lust," Rabbeinu Bachaya has this to say regarding its historical relevance:

> "The difference between the earlier generations and us as concerns the trait of restraint is just this: men such as Hanoch, Noach, Avraham, Yitzchak, and Ya'akov…maintained a clear mind and yet a weak evil inclination, which therefore led them to follow after their intellects. As such, a minimum amount of *mitzvot* sufficed for them, together with the purity of their faith, to serve God fully and completely...They had no need for asceticism, which departs from the Golden Mean that the Torah prescribes.
>
> But when their descendents went down to Egypt...their sensual lust strengthened and their desire increased until ultimately their evil inclination prevailed over their reason. Hence they stood in need of a mode of restraint to counter their desire and help them

resist their evil inclination. God therefore gave them *mitzvot* that were to be obeyed by divine decree as a set minimum level of restraint, fitting not only to their capacity but even lower" (Gate of Restraint, Chapter 7).[3]

In the generations preceding the Torah, the relationship of the body to the soul was such that essentially the soul retained the upper hand. The mind, as it were, held sway over the heart. In such a spiritual condition, man needed very little self-restraint to serve God correctly. Those elements within his psyche that distracted him from his divine service required nary an effort to overcome.

But as impurity slowly crept into the heart of man, it became necessary for him to muster more effort to control his own inclinations. Therefore, by the time the Jews left Egypt, they needed much more spiritual instruction to condition themselves to the service of God. While their ancestors found it possible to do so with only a few *mitzvot*, the Jews of the Exodus needed literally hundreds.

To this insight, Seforno would just add that after the Sin of the Golden Calf we needed yet a few more. Having become more susceptible to impurity, the Jews required a further mode of restraint (in the form of *kashrut* and family purity laws), as food and sexual pleasure, while in themselves not negative at all, became major distractions from the true purpose of existence.[4]

---

[3] I am indebted to Rabbi Isaac Bernstein *z"l* of London for showing me this source.

[4] There are several questions that Seforno leaves in the open: Based on his thesis would there not be a need for even more *mitzvot* in our days since the principle of *yeridot hadorot* applies today to an even greater extent? Maybe the 613 *mitzvot* in the Torah are insufficient? Or does the Seforno hold the opinion that the 613 are sufficient even for generations that fall even lower? Does he believe that rabbinical law overcomes this problem? Moreover, since it is well know that the prohibitions on Shabbat are derived from the

---

work which was done to build the *Mishkan*, would this mean that Shabbat would have been observed differently were it not for the incident with the golden calf? Or is the deduction from the work to build the *Mishkan* only an *asmachta*, a "rabbinical leaning on," and not the real reason at all? See Mishnah, Shabbat 7:2, and associated commentaries.

Finally there is the question about the obligation to observe the *mitzvot* of the Torah in the messianic age. Is there still any need for this? Or will the *mitzvot* still apply on a higher and more perfect level? See my booklet: *The Torah as God's Mind*, Bep Ron Foundation, Jerusalem, 1988.

See also: Marc B. Shapiro, *The Limits of Orthodox Theology: Maimonides' Thirteen Principles Reappraised*, The Littman Library of Jewish Civilization, Oxford, 2004, chapter 8.

Chapter 6

RELIGIOUS AUTHENTICITY AND WONDER IN AND BEYOND HALACHA

THINGS THAT ARE ALIVE constantly move and grow. Organic matter that fails to grow, shift, and move, decays and eventually dies. So it is with the human being. A man who does not strive to grow and transform himself, who does not live with passion and excitement, is a man who is not fully living. Such men merely exist and survive on our planet. Like all of God's creations, Man must experience seasons of his soul – cycles of change and renewal.

Jewish philosophy sees God primarily as a Creator: "Every day He (re)creates the works of the beginning." The Jew declares this every morning during his prayers. And since Man is "created in the image of God," it follows that man, in his essence, must also be a creator.[1] A man who is not constantly engaged in creative endeavors, denies his nature.

The role of religion is to facilitate the blooming of the soul, and to prevent Man from descending into spiritual stagnation. Genuine religion should implant a consciousness in men that helps them actualize their creative energy, thus allowing them to emulate their Creator at the highest level. One of the most powerful ways that religions accomplish this critical goal, is by training their followers in the art of wonderment.

Mask Logic

In a fascinating passage in the Torah concerning Moshe's descent from Sinai, we learn about one of his most remarkable initiatives:

---

[1] *Bereshit* 1.25.

> "When Moshe descended from Mount Sinai, with the Tablets of Testimony in Moshe's hands; as he descended from the mountain, Moshe did not realize that the skin on his face became radiant when he spoke to Him. Aaron and all the children of Israel saw Moshe, and behold!, Moshe's skin had become radiant; and they feared to approach him. Moshe called to them and they came to him – Aaron and all the princes of the assembly – and Moshe spoke to them.
>
> After that, all the children of Israel would approach, and he would command them regarding everything that God had spoken to him on Mount Sinai. After Moshe finished speaking to them, he placed a mask on his face. When Moshe came before God to speak with Him, he would remove the mask until his departure, and then he would leave and recount to the children of Israel what he was commanded. And the children would see Moshe's face – that the skin of Moshe's face was radiant. Moshe would put the mask back on his face until he came to speak with Him" (*Shemot* 34: 29–35).

What was the purpose of this mask? Why did Moshe need to hide his radiance? It seems that Moshe concealed his shining face when he spoke with the people. This would make sense since the people, and even his own brother Aaron, were afraid to approach him. The glow from Moshe's face overwhelmed and paralyzed the people who beheld it. As such, one might conclude that the main purpose of the mask was to allow the people to be close to Moshe without fear or intimidation.

A deeper analysis of the text, however, suggests a very different reading. A second look reveals that Moshe actually removes the mask in the presence of the B'nei Yisrael, and puts it back on his face only *after* speaking with them. The classical work, *Bina Le'itim*, provides a fascinating insight into this episode.[2] What was God's intention when he caused Moshe's face to become illuminated? Moshe did not need to be convinced of the fact that he had received the word of God. Therefore, the rays of light emanating from Moshe's face must have conveyed a necessary message to the people regarding Moshe's religious integrity, authenticity, and authority. Above all, Moshe's incandescent countenance was meant to invoke a religious "joie de vivre" in the hearts of the Jewish people, and to thoroughly energize them with spiritual verve.

The radiance allowed the Jewish people to be newly inspired every time they looked at the face of their leader and teacher. The supernatural glow ideally would have kept the Jews in a permanent state of religious amazement. This was critical since God communicated His word through Moshe over a period of time. Thus, Moshe's face reminded the people of the source of the commandments, and ensured that they received God's laws with the right attitude. The awe they felt while listening to a man whose face was alight with spiritual energy, allowed them to experience each communication as if it were the first – with a sense of novelty and excitement. God's messages captivated them completely, as Moshe delivered the Word in all its nuanced complexity.

Of course, we all know that human beings can become desensitized to astonishing stimuli very quickly. How many of us still marvel at our ability to speak to our friends via cell phone? How many of us are awed each time we profit from the convenience of the Internet? So too, if the people saw Moshe walking around the camp with a radiant face all the time, the effect would have worn off. Only by revealing his face sporadically, on special occasions, could the phenomenon continue to astonish, as it did when Moshe first came

---

[2] *Bina Le'itim, parashat Ki Tisa.*

down from the mountain. For the radiance to stay radiant, it had to be hidden. Familiarity breeds contempt!

So when Moshe walked through the camp, he wore his mask.[3] In this way, the people never got the chance to become desensitized to the experience of hearing direct communication from the Creator of the Universe, nor did they doubt their teacher's legitimacy.

The Temple Gates

The prophet Yechezkel saw the following vision concerning the third and future Temple:

> And on the Mo'adim (festivals) when the Amei Ha'aretz (common people) came before the Lord (in the future Temple) – whoever enters by the northern gate to bow low, shall leave by the south gate, and whoever enters by the south gate shall leave through the northern gate. They shall not go back through the same gate by which they came in, but shall go out by the opposite one (46:9)

Rabbi Jonathan Eibeshutz in his classic commentary on *Pirke Avot* asks what purpose it served to have people enter and leave through different gates. He writes, "God was particular that man should not see the same gate (of the Temple) twice. Lest he see the gate as he sees the door of his house."[4]

If people became overly familiar with the House of God, it would cease to serve one of its most valuable purposes. The Temple invoked in man a sense of great wonder. While inside the first temples, the Jewish people witnessed many miraculous occurrences that sensitized them to the hidden miracles manifested in their

---

[3] It seems that Moshe's mask was a kind of hair-thin covering which did not completely hide his face.

[4] Rabbi Jonathan Eibeshutz on *Pirke Avot* 5:7.

everyday lives.[5] This sensitization process began with the Temple gates.

An object we observe twice, already begins to lose its aura. In spiritual matters, this presents a serious problem. Since even a second encounter carries the seeds of familiarity and ultimately boredom, one should (for the sake of his connection with the Creator of the universe) try never to see anything more than once. Of course, the best way to combat this problem, since we obviously must all traverse the same paths many times as we go about our routines, is to see things always with a new eye and a sharper understanding. Since we cannot provide ourselves with an ever-new environment to stave off our ennui, we must change our perception and ourselves so that we notice new aspects, details, and depths, in the things we've seen on numerous occasions before. The Temple was the ultimate worldview elevator; after being inside, it was virtually impossible not to see the world in a completely new light.

Rabbi Jonathan Eibeshutz sees this issue at the center of the Golden Calf incident.[6] Somehow the Israelites got too familiar with Moshe and became desensitized to his unprecedented greatness and religious authenticity. They therefore desired a new spiritual conduit, and believed erroneously that they could generate it themselves. This attempt to replace Moshe was their very undoing. Had they made themselves into deeper perceivers of reality, instead, they would have recognized that below the surface, their leader Moshe was a spiritual giant. Precisely because the Jewish people failed to appreciate what they already had, God blessed Moshe later with his astonishing facial radiance.

Not only did the people take Moshe for granted, the community also lost their awe of God. In a sense, the Golden Calf was also an

---

[5] Ibid.

[6] Rabbi Jonathan Eibeshutz, ibid.

attempt to replace God with a new, and therefore more exciting, spiritual entity.[7]

Frequent Miracles

In his *Michtav Me-Eliyahu*, Rabbi Eliyahu Eliezer Dessler discusses the modern world's conception of the phenomenon we call "nature." He explains that modern man, as a rule, has come to believe that the laws of nature are fully explainable by science. This, however, is a farce, and both religious thinkers and also many great scientists agree that science is in fact extremely limited in its explanatory powers. According to Rabbi Dessler, the laws of nature do not really exist as such, but are only indicative of the way the universe interacts with the human perceptual apparatus.[8]

Moreover, what we perceive as hard and fast laws of nature, are actually the result of God's miraculous re-creation in every moment. It is *frequency* that leads us to put our faith in the laws of nature. After all how do we discover these laws? When we observe a phenomenon enough times and see that it repeats itself constantly and consistently, we form a belief that this is the way the world behaves. But what we really observe in such cases, is the frequent repetition of a miracle.

If during the course of human history, only a single comet had ever streaked across the night sky, we would be as much astonished by that anomaly as we are by the splitting of the Red Sea in Moshe's days. Likewise, if we witnessed a constant repetition of the Red Sea parting on a regular cycle, we would ultimately conclude that splitting oceans are part of the natural course of events, and as such we would explain the phenomenon within the framework of some newly

---

[7] For a full explanation of this issue see my *Between Silence and Speech, Essays in Jewish Thought*, Jason Aronson Inc, Northvale, New Jersey, London, 1995, pp. 1–12.

[8] Rabbi Eliyahu Eliezer Dessler, *Michtav Me-Eliyahu*, volume one, p. 177.

derived natural law. And such is the case with all natural laws, that they do not really explain the underlying causes for anything. Rather, they simply describe in a logical way, the regular processes that happen around us.[9]

Science is Tentative

Professor Karl Popper, one of the great philosophers of science in the 20th century, draws attention to the fact that the laws of nature are not reducible to elementary experiments, as far as logic is concerned. The reason is that we can never test our theories completely. The truth of the statement that "*all* copper conducts electricity," really depends on our ability to check *all* the copper that exists in the universe. Clearly then, within all statements of natural law, there is some element of faith involved. Popper writes regarding scientific knowledge that, "We do not know, but we guess. And our guess is guided by an unscientific belief that there are laws that we can reveal and discover… It is not the possession of irrefutable truth that makes the scientist, but rather an ongoing search for the truth... Knowing something for sure is not given to us. Our knowledge is a critical guess, a net of hypotheses, a texture of presumption."[10] Every scientific statement is tentative. It can be confirmed, but only to a limited extent. "The old scientific concept of absolute knowledge, is nothing but an idol."[11]

---

[9] It has been argued that the Big Bang theory would on the basis of the above not be "scientific" since it lacks frequency. Scientists have however argued that the theory is based on the fact that one is able to trace this moment back because of the physical effects it had on the universe which we continue to experience. It that sense it does rely on frequency.

[10] Karl Popper, *Logic der Forschung*, Tubingen, 1976, p. xxv, German.

[11] Ibid., pp. 221–225.

In a dramatic statement, the famous scientist Max Planck provides us with a completely different and equally important viewpoint on what scientific inquiry is essentially:

> "The feeling of wonderment is the source and inexhaustible fountainhead of the desire for knowledge. It drives the child irresistibly on to solve the mystery, and if in his attempt he encounters a causal relationship, he will not tire of repeating the same experiment ten times – a hundred times – in order to taste the thrill of discovery over and over again. The reason why the adult no longer wonders is not because he has solved the riddle of life, but because he has grown accustomed to the laws governing this world picture. But the problem of why these particular laws, and no others, hold, remains for him just as amazing and inexplicable as for the child. He who does not comprehend this situation, misconstrues its profound significance, and he who has reached the stage where he no longer wonders about anything, merely demonstrates that he has lost the art of reflective reasoning."[12]

Dogmatic Fallacy

The surest way to suppress our ability to understand the meaning of religion is to take our world for granted. Likewise, one of the most important tasks of genuine religion is to protest against such an attitude. Modern man has fallen into the trap of believing that everything can be explained. Even if he doesn't understand what he perceives around him (e.g., light, life, death, weather patterns, etc.), he has faith in the power of Science to reveal, order, and master nature. Since he believes that all enigmas can be solved, modern man

[12] Max Planck, *Scientific Biography*, NY, 1949, pp. 91–93.

considers amazement to be a function of primitive ignorance. Few people fully understand the fallacy of this worldview.

> "The history of European thought, even to the present day, has been tainted by a fatal misunderstanding. It may be termed the Dogmatic Fallacy. The error consists in the persuasion that we are capable of producing notions which are adequately defined in respect to the complexity of relationship required for their illustration in the real world. Canst thou by searching describe the universe? Except perhaps for the simpler notions of arithmetic, even our most familiar ideas, seemingly obvious, are infected with this incurable vagueness. Our right understanding of the methods of intellectual progress depends on keeping in mind this characteristic of our thoughts… During the medieval epoch in Europe, the theologians were the chief sinners in respect to dogmatic finality. During the last three centuries, their pre-eminence in this habit was inherited by the men of science."[13]

Life is only worth living when one lives in wonder, because consciousness of existence and all its mysteries, elevates and gives meaning to our experience. Science and reason cannot explain anything to its core. Physics can tell us about the Big Bang, but not "why" the Big Bang occurred, or "why" it happened. And so too for all the other "whys." Why is life propagated through the union of sperm and egg? Why are there seven colors in a rainbow? Why are things this way and not any other? To ask the deeper "why," is to wonder. And man was given his superior mind in order that he should spend his life in a perpetual state of wonderment. With a little concentration, man can and must reach the recognition that everything, without exception, is baffling, including the very fact that

[13] Alfred Northern Whitehead, *Adventures of Ideas*, NY, 1933, p. 185.

he can be baffled. Even the act of thinking should amaze us. Our ability to reason scientifically is a complete mystery, which of course implies that those who faithfully believe that science will one day develop a complete theory of everything have "lost the art of reflective reasoning."

A *Bracha* is a Statement of Astonishment

To remain in the state of appropriate wonderment, we must develop a capacity to look deeper and deeper, so that we can always find something new in everything we encounter. Without developing our ear for music, we become bored at hearing a composition for the second and third times. One does not gain a greater appreciation for a painting by simply staring at it. In Judaism, we hone our ability to perceive the transcendent in our everyday reality by making a *bracha* (blessing) whenever we partake of food or drink. Jews make *brachot*, which are statements of astonishment and recognition of the amazing complexity that surrounds us, whenever we see a new fruit tree, wear a new garment, smell a pleasant fragrance, etc. The *bracha*, when said with concentration and feeling, ensures that we experience each day as something entirely new. Even when a Jew relieves himself, he afterwards takes time to thank God for giving him such a well-functioning body. This is indeed one of the most important goals of traditional Jewish practice: to experience spirituality in commonplace deeds.

In a remarkable observation the rabbis declared: "Redemption and the earning of bread may be compared to each other. There is [as much] wonder in earning bread as there is wonder in redeeming the world." Just as the earning of bread takes place every day, so too redemption take place every day, because fundamentally redemption means the revelation of an underlying reality which has yet to be noticed by humanity. But Rabbi Yehoshua ben Levi added: "*The earning of bread is a greater wonder than the division of the Red Sea,*" because to him, the daily repetition of a miracle is more impressive than the one-time miracle of the splitting of the Red Sea.[14]

The Mysterium

Such an attitude should however not become a cushion for the lazy intellect. Just because our ability to understand reality is necessarily limited does not mean that we shouldn't seek to know all we can. Where analysis is possible, we must analyze. And where doubt is legitimate, we must doubt. All the while, though, we must remain cognizant of the fact that ultimately, we all reside within a great mysterium.

Emanuel Kant, in his masterpiece *Critique of Practical Reason,* expresses a similar point:

> "Two things fill the mind with ever new and increasing admiration and awe the more often and the more steadily we reflect on them: the starry heavens above, and the moral law within... The countless multitudes of galaxies annihilates, as it were, my importance as an animal creature, which after it has been for a short time provided with a vital power (one knows not how) must again give back the matter of which it was formed to the planet it inhabits, a mere speck in the universe. The second, on the contrary, infinitely elevates my worth as an intelligence by my personality, in which the moral law reveals to me a life independent of animal-nature, and even of the whole sensible world – at least so far as may be inferred from the destination

[14] *Bereshit Rabbah*, 20:22 and *Pesachim* 118a.

assigned to my existence by this law, a destination not restricted to conditions and limits of this life, but reaching into the infinite."[15]

Coerced by Sinai

The Talmud in tractate Shabbat 88a, relates a serious dilemma the children of Israel encountered when they received the Torah at Mt. Sinai. The incident is one of the most difficult parts of the Talmud to comprehend, and commentators throughout the ages have struggled with its meaning.

In anticipation of God's revelation, the children of Israel "placed themselves at the mountain" (*Shemot* 19:17). The Talmud, an extremely exacting grammarian when it comes to God's words, states that in reality the text does not say that they placed themselves *at* the mountain, but rather *under* (*tachtit)* the mountain. The unusual phraseology gives rise to an allegorical interpretation of its meaning. The sages suggest that God "took the mountain and turned it on its top," and threatened the Israelites. "If you accept the Torah (and its commandments), then you will live, but if you do not, there will be your burial place" – right under the mountain!

The Talmudic sage, Rabbi Acha bar Ya'akov, makes a surprising observation that creates major theological problems. Rather than just accept that God, who is the Lord of the Universe, can make any condition on his human creations, Rabbi Acha bar Ya'akov responds to this story with great consternation. "From here we must deduce a strong objection against the very giving of the Torah!" Rashi here explains, that forcing the Israelites to accept the Torah could be considered unjust and morally objectionable. Why would God force the Jewish people into a religious commitment under duress? Is the Torah not a covenant? And does its status as covenant not imply that

---

15 Emanuel Kant, *Critique of Practical Reason*, translated by Abbott, London, 1889, p. 260.

both parties should freely agree to its terms without any kind of coercion?

This observation however begs the question: Is *obedience* to God not at the very root of religious life? Why would Rabbi Acha bar Ya'akov, who spent his entire life trying to understand and obey God's directives for mankind, object to God forcing His will on the Jews at Sinai? We could ask a completely different question: Why does God, who created the Universe, and gave man his role in it, need to establish a covenant to get people to do His will? Why give us any choice in the matter at all?

The most surprising part of the whole discussion is the Talmud's response to Rabbi Acha bar Ya'akov. After agreeing with the rabbi's objections, the Talmud says that the matter was rectified many hundreds of years later at the time of Mordechai and Esther (i.e., in the Purim narrative), when the Jews, after being saved from Haman's plot, accepted the Torah out of their own free will, thus rendering our covenant with God fully legitimate and in good faith from all sides.

Boredom as Coercion

Lying beneath this give-and-take is our original problem of boredom and the need to experience a sense of wonder. After coming out of Egypt in a barrage of miraculous plagues, and then witnessing the splitting of the Red Sea, and eating manna, and experiencing a whole host of supernatural phenomena, the Israelites were not in the best position to really appreciate the profundity of the giving of the Torah at Sinai. Revelation for that generation, was the status quo. And so Sinai becomes a paradox.

On one level God's entrance into the physical world in such an all-encompassing way, totally overwhelmed the Israelites so that they felt as though they were forced to accept the Torah. On another level, they were desensitized to an extent, and thus lacked the capacity to recognize each divine Word as a unique expression of God's greatness. There was a deficiency of enthusiasm for the Torah and its commandments, which implies that they did not accept it as *completely* free beings. Receiving the Torah as a free will choice does not mean having an option to refuse (because that is simply not an option), but rather to recognize the *mitzvot* as a source of tremendous joy and wonderment.

In the days of Mordechai and Esther, when open miracles no longer took place, the Jews were able to appreciate fully the wondrous way in which they were saved. They stood in awe of God since their normal existence was so routine. As such, the miracle of their salvation affected them like the radiance of Moshe's face affected their ancestors years before. Ironically, those who witnessed more, saw less; and those who witnessed less, actually saw more.

The Jewish custom to wear masks on Purim, when Jews celebrate the miracle of their salvation from Haman's genocidal plot, is therefore not unfounded. By concealing our faces, we remind ourselves of the need to see miracles hiding behind commonplace events. Metaphorically, on Purim, we don the mask that Moshe wore.

Futuric Wonder

For Judaism to remain a religion of wonder, we must keep an eye on the future. All living is living into the future, but of course, no future is completely open. The events to come are deeply rooted in the past. Judaism, like most religions, has a strong tendency to celebrate the past. After all, the Jewish people's greatest glory and triumph took place many centuries ago. It is only logical that Jews cling to these events. A Judaism without historic memory is therefore inconceivable.

Jewish practice must remind us that God created the world in six days, and that He rested on the seventh. It must focus on Avraham's remarkable personality, on the Israelites' miraculous exodus from Egypt, and obviously on its most transcendent moment – the giving of the Torah at Sinai. Since our tradition derives from events that took place in the past, there is a strong urge to place the emphasis in Judaism on the past. And yet, to do so would be to misconstrue the very essence of our religion. However significant the past may be, its value lies primarily in its ability to inform the future. To stay genuine, the epic Jewish experience must be re-lived, now and in the future, giving birth to exciting elements that continue to create wonder and anticipation.

Observant Jews, therefore, never memorialize their great history. Rather, they celebrate the events of their people's distant past as if they took place in the present day. During Pesach, the Jew sits at the Seder table and tells the story of the exodus from Egypt is such a way that he re-experiences it. He is obligated to create an atmosphere in which he and his family feel as though they themselves were slaves in Egypt, and who are now able to enjoy freedom. The famous Chassidic saying that Pesach is not so much a festival about how the Jews got out of Egypt, but how Egypt and its mentality gets out of the Jews, beautifully illustrates the point. Halachically, Pesach has to be experienced in a way that transcends history, and thereby illuminates the present.

Pesach is also a celebration of the future and the messianic times to come, since in its essence, Pesach is the festival of redemption. This is one of the great secrets of Judaism's success. Our traditions allow us to travel through time, realizing a history that has yet to take place. Religious Jews live in a constant state of anticipation and wonder. On Shabbat, while sitting at home in a state of peace, without the need to do any work, they experience a taste of what the messianic days will be like, when everyone will sit "under his own palm tree." On Succoth, they live under the open sky in an unstable structure, the Succah, to experience another aspect of the messianic age, when we will all have total clarity about the fact that God provides for our security. Miracles that are already celebrated, but have not yet taken place, will always stay new and cause wonder.

Withdrawal

It is here that we find problems in the contemporary Jewish religious situation. Over the years, Judaism has shifted to a Tradition-centric religion, focusing primarily on the past and ignoring the promise of a messianic future. Without an eye on its redemptive goal as a global spiritual revolutionary movement, Judaism has become somewhat withdrawn from the world. This is most apparent when we compare stories of the great sages with the situation today. Many stories in the Talmud demonstrate how much the sages were involved in their communities. They dwelled in inns, conversed with the peasants, learned with the simpletons. They were involved in commerce, even politics. Of course, they dedicated many years of their lives to intensive learning, during which they sometimes withdrew from society, but always with an intention to return. Traditionally, withdrawal was seen only as a means.

The great Chassidic Rebbes interacted with the common man, became farmers, cut wood, and looked after babies when their mothers had to leave home. This was not just due to their intense love for humanity, but also because they realized that one must be involved in day to day life to stay religiously fresh. At the same time, they understood that retreat could be useful for meditation, after which they could return with a greater sense of wonder. Through withdrawal, they were able, like Moshe, to remove the masks of complacency and see the world with wonder, always from different points of view. This allowed them to be highly successful leaders. They were able to move Judaism in a direction of renewal and vibrant life, something which their Lithuanian counterparts, who developed the Mussar movement, did not accomplish to the same extent. While the Mussar movement, with its emphasis on character development, stayed a small movement, Chassidut moved millions of Jews and created empires based on lively religious experience.

Expect the Unexpected

For Judaism to stay vibrant, it must develop an atmosphere that fosters creativity. Without growth and creative energy, religions fall away into obscurity. Everything in this world that remains static, ultimately decays. Judaism must always be open to the unexpected. This, after all, is the deepest manifestation of the awareness of God's living presence. To embrace the potential for upheaval, means recognizing that so long as God runs the world, nothing is predictable. Such an attitude properly reflects the reality of God's involvement in the world.

Jewish history is full of unexpected moments coming from unexpected settings at the most unexpected times. Redemption does not spring from where we seek it, but often from situations where we expect it the least. For example, Moshe, our redeemer, stuttered. Who would ever have imagined that he would become the leader responsible for bringing down the mighty Egyptian Empire? Moshe's background logically should have caused him to side with Pharaoh in his fight with the Jews. After all, Moshe was raised by Pharaoh's daughter in Pharaoh's own house, and received a thoroughly Egyptian (i.e., anti-Jewish) education. Who would ever think that such a man would rise to become the redeemer of Israel? So too the Mashiach, our ultimate redeemer, will not come as the result of a natural process, but as a sudden interference of God in the natural order of things. The Mashiach can come in the blink of an eye, when the world least expects him. This is the wonder of the Mashiach, an element that Judaism must surely maintain if it wants to stay alive to witness its fruition.

Authentic Novelty

Although there is a very real need for religions to be able to see things in a new way, one must be wary of novelty for its own sake. One of the greatest tragedies in modern Jewish life is that the call for novelty often has little to do with authentic religiosity. Most of the time, changes are introduced for the sake of social accommodation. The Reform movement, and to a lesser extent Conservative Judaism, were much more motivated by social and economic factors than by the need for renewed Jewish spirituality. While we will not deny that some of its spokesmen were concerned about a perceived lack of spirituality in traditional Judaism, most of the social changes in Judaism have arisen from a desire to partake in the pleasures of Western culture, and to gain entrance to the country club that is "modernity."

Reading the history of German Jewry of the nineteenth century it is clear that Reform Judaism became a new option *after* many Jews (in pre-war Germany and other European countries) had already abandoned traditional Judaism. The Reform Movement served as a retroactive justification *de jure* of what had long been the case *de facto*. As such, it did not add anything of real substance to Jewish spiritual life, which is clear from the fact that it has not produced enlightened *religious* leaders. Neither did it create a spiritual movement, as was the case with the early Chassidim.

Divine Revelation and Wonder

Many modern thinkers argue that revelation is an impossibility. They explain away the events recorded in the Torah by claiming that our forefathers misconstrued natural phenomena as revelation due to their simple way of thinking and their lack of philosophical and scientific knowledge. A deeper look, however, may reveal a very different picture.

Scientific reasoning, while tremendously important, also has a down side. As mentioned before, scientific inquiry depends on laws that necessarily exclude the possibility for exceptions. Nature's general constancy is what allows for scientific inquiry, and for its results to be so powerful. But, revelation is revelation only in so far as it demonstrates an existence beyond the consistent order of things. For revelation to serve its purpose (i.e., to make a big impression on those who experience it) it must be extra-ordinary and preferably unprecedented. And so it is the "nature" of revelation to elude scientific inquiry. The moment it can be repeated or understood, the miracle loses much of its significance.

Still, we must be able to trust that what we experience in such moments, is real. Unfortunately, authentic revelation lacks resemblance to other kinds of experience, and since we are trained to think in terms of categories and sameness, we adopt a Western world-view in which the extra-ordinary is impossible. Revelation is not so much rejected because of any proper logical reason, but rather because our minds have been indoctrinated to believe that what cannot be replicated, should not be taken seriously. But this is a logical fallacy. Just because something cannot happen again, does not give us a reason to claim that it could not have happened. For example, there will never be another person like you in the world, with the same genetic information and life experiences. Yet, you exist.

You, and every other human being you see, are walking, talking proofs that one-time-only events can and do happen.

Mind Closing

Belief in revelation depends on our openness to wonder. The *a priori* rejection of revelation, based on the fact that it cannot be proven via scientific investigation, is not a sign of progressive thinking, but rather of an intellectual and spiritual stagnancy. It is too easy to be lulled into a sense that the well-defined laws and ordered progression of events constitute all that reality has to offer. In the meantime, we become mentally shut off from what can happen suddenly and without precedent. Because our forefathers were still open to the possibility of unexpected occurrences, they therefore had little reason to doubt the possibility of revelation on a grand scale. It was not their intellectual primitivism but their open-mindedness – their willingness to see what was, rather than what they expected or understood – which gave them the capacity to wonder, and therefore to trust their belief in revelation.

Novelty and Law

Novelty poses a problem for law. The application of law would be much easier if the world were stagnant and consisted of more limited variety and endless repetition. The real difficulty arises when situations change radically, because suddenly the established precedents fail to provide enough relevant insight to make definitive judgements. In such cases, the lawmakers are forced to become creative. Such a situation exists now for the orthodox Jewish world. The profound changes in the state of the world and of world Jewry since the emancipation, and even more since the holocaust and the establishment of the State of Israel, demand creative thinking in order to render judgements on unprecedented halachic issues.

In the past, many halachic decisions were made locally. With the re-entrance of Jews into world history through the emancipation and the establishment of a Jewish State, halachic authorities were thrust into a new era, which forced them to rule on decisions of life and death on a national level. This was never before the case in the Diaspora. The halachic arguments in Israel over whether or not to relinquish parts of the so-called West Bank for security reasons, is a good case in point. Such a profound shift in such a short time-span, means that in some cases, the law has not entirely caught up with the street. As a result, we find that it is possible to find convincing proofs for completely opposing views, which augments the confusion, especially in matters of national importance.

Spiritual Crisis and Halacha

Even so, the greatest problem in the Jewish world today is its haunting spiritual crisis. Unfortunately, spiritual crises are the most difficult to quell, as they concern life in its totality, and therefore demand a response that provides a personal course of action and thought, which will necessarily transcend the inherent limitations of a purely legalistic approach. A solution to our spiritual crisis must allow the unseen to enter the visible world, giving man the ability to go beyond the realms of the definable, perceivable, and demonstrable. The answer lies in our ability to cultivate wonder. But over the years this part of the Jewish tradition has been increasingly neglected, ignored and even denigrated.

A large percentage of the Talmud is composed of aggadita, the non-legal side of the Jewish wisdom tradition. The spiritual grandeur of the aggadic text, its magnificent understanding of Jewishness and Jewish history, and its keen insight into the nature of religion and the religious personality, are precisely what would reinvigorate the Jewish world. Unfortunately, the majority of conventional *yeshivot* do not focus on these sections of the Talmud. The result is that our most talented youth emerge from the *yeshivot* unable to guide the vast majority of Jews. In addition, many of these higher Jewish learning institutions have become sapped of real religious fervor since they do not incorporate the *weltanschauung* set forth by the aggadita. This is regrettable since one can often understand the depths of Halacha and ensure its proper application *only after* one has an awareness of the deeper messages developed in the world of the aggadita.[16]

Halachic Theology

We see in Tanach that when King David and the later kings had to decide on national matters, they were guided both by Halacha and also by an understanding of Judaism as a way of life based on a theology in which God remains extremely active. Deeply religious concerns weighed heavily in their thought processes in political matters (i.e., the state and its security). Of course, for the Jewish Kings, statecraft was a means to bring the people of Israel closer to God. And this is really the point – that the leaders of our distant past were able to integrate fully, the implementation of Halacha with the spiritual growth and aspirations of the nation. Halachic decisions helped connect our people with God's divine presence. Israel's legal affairs were simultaneously (on a deeper level) journeys into the highest spiritual realms, generating spiritual breakthroughs in which the world and God came a little closer, which in turn aroused feelings of religious amazement and fervor. In this way the Halacha stayed fresh, and was therefore able to deal with new issues and unprecedented circumstances.

In our days, halachic authorities should perhaps call upon Jewish religious thinkers to help them integrate the experience of wonder

[16] See my *The Written and Oral Torah, A Comprehensive Introduction*, Jason Aronson Inc, Northvale, New Jersey, 1989, pp. 167–192.

and universal Jewish values into their decision-making process. Their halachic rulings would then emanate from a broader and more inclusive base. While pluralism for its own sake is not necessarily a good thing, in this case, having a wide variety of highly sophisticated and broad thinking people of many different flavors take part in the discussion, could add legitimacy to the judge's final ruling and ensure that it is more widely accepted among Jews from across the entire spectrum of religious observance. The Jewish people as a whole will come to feel that the halachic decisions coming down from its leaders are as wise as they can possibly be, which is probably the most we can ask for.

Halachic decisions must be made in the spirit of a living covenant, with the recognition that each judgement serves as a link in the ongoing rejuvenation of God's word. The Halacha should guide us in our attempts to manifest God's will, while living in a constantly changing world that continues to astonish us.

Chapter 7
On Halacha as the Art of Amazement

In the way that man observes the world and interacts with it, he reveals one of the most surprising and impressive sides to all of human existence: the faculty of appreciation. When walking through a landscape he can be overwhelmed by its beauty. Wondering at the sky, standing at the seashore, or viewing the sunset, he becomes aware of an inner, uplifting experience that he cannot verbalize. Enjoying the music of Mozart, Beethoven, or Paganini, man can be lifted to unprecedented heights. Through the constant search for beauty, harmony, conformity, and so forth, man confirms his unique place in this universe. But even in the "small moments" of man's life, he shows an unusual appreciation for his surroundings. When choosing the interior of his home or the color and style of his clothes, he will carefully select colors, patterns, and specific combinations. Many hours, if not days and months (or years), are spent on this endeavor. For most people this is far from a waste of time but rather a deep emotional need that enriches their lives.

Things must "go well," flow into each other, and create a picture of great harmony, tranquility, and beauty. One blotch of paint will not inspire us, but a certain combination of them definitely does. One musical note is boring, but the flowing of many of them within a certain pattern will make a symphony that can bring thousands of listeners to exaltation. Art collectors will pay large amounts of money to become the owners of paintings that are often no larger than a few square centimeters. Some paintings are valued at millions of dollars and are viewed by hundreds of thousands of human beings, who are often prepared to travel long distances to view them. The world of haute couture has, for thousands of years, produced an infinite amount of elegant (and not so elegant) garments of all kinds and fashions. Instead of man tiring of all these efforts and getting bored, he is deeply involved in all this, searching for every possible new way to make sure that beauty and novelty will always be with him.

How Did We Get Like That?

Let us ask: How did we get like that? Rudolf Otto and many others have already made us realize that we cannot adequately explain why we enjoy music or fall in love with a painting or the seashore.[1] Indeed, what is there about beauty that makes it beautiful? What is there so great about a van Gogh, or the music of Beethoven? Is there not a certain absurdity to all this? How is it that we can hear more than one musical note at a time? And why is it that we do not just hear the different notes together but also apprehend them as a unity? We somehow grasp them. We are conscious of the music and its beauty. There is indeed a faculty called appreciation. But what is this faculty made of? The American philosopher G.N.M. Tyrrel (in his *Grades of Significance*), writing about "reading," reminds the reader of this most miraculous faculty of man:[2]

> A book we will suppose, has fallen into the hands of intelligent beings who know nothing of what writing and printing mean, but they are accustomed to dealing with the external relationships of things. They try to find out the laws of the book, which for them mean the principles governing the order in which the letters are arranged.... [T]hey will think they have discovered the laws of the book when they formulated certain rules governing the external

---

[1] Rudolf, Otto, *The Idea of the Holy* (London, 1923; rev. ed. 1929).

[2] London, 1939; quoted by E.F. Schumacher, *A Guide for the Perplexed* (New York: Harper Colophon Books, 1978), p. 42.

> relationships of the letters. That each word and each sentence expresses a meaning will never dawn on them because their background of thought is made up of concepts which deal only with external relationships, and explanations to them means solving the puzzle of these external relationships.... Their methods will never reach the grade of significance which contains the idea of meanings.

Why do we associate sounds with meaning? How is it that meaningless shapes are capable of triggering within us the concept of meaning? Perhaps the most outstanding example of man's mysterious nature is the experience of love. If we could imagine a creature from outer space looking at the human body, what would he see? Probably one of the most repulsive creations walking around in the cosmos. "Deformed" organs such as protrusions of flesh hanging on both sides of some kind of roundness or enlarged balloon on top of the human body. In the middle of this ball, called a head, there is another extension placed between two items of glass, and below, a hole into which man disposes of all sorts of substances (which by outer space standards have a most offensive taste!). Legs and arms will be described in most uncomplimentary terms. Most astonishing of all would no doubt be the fact that these "monstrous" creations fall in love with each other, fight wars because of jealousy, and like to have intimate relationships that result in producing even more of these unsightly creatures. Why, indeed, do we not consider music an abhorrent experience, a Rembrandt painting the ravings of a hideous human creativity, or lovemaking as a most repulsive act?

Amazement

This, in fact, touches on the very core of religion and the problem of secularism. Western civilization has a very specific approach to life. It is highly pragmatic. Matters are basically seen from a purely utilitarian point of view. Everything is measured by result-getting standards. What matters is whether things "work." Humans have become tool-making creatures for whom the world is a gigantic toolbox for the satisfaction of their needs. Satisfaction, luxury, and pleasure are man's goals. Everything is calculated, and there is supreme faith in statistics.

This has possibly caused the greatest problem of our times: the tragedy of existential indifference, missing out on exactly that which is no doubt the most exciting side of life – the mysterium tremendum that lies behind all existence, after every move man makes, behind every human experience. It is the invisible part of life where the real flow of life runs, that which the five senses cannot grasp or touch. Modern man takes notice of what surrounds him and tells himself that everything will be explained. Man looks to the skeleton but does not see the content and the essence. Maurice Nicoll describes this very well when he discusses the fact that humans cannot even see themselves or their fellowmen:[3]

> We can all see another person's body directly. We see the lips moving, the eyes opening and shutting, the lines of the mouth and face changing, and the body expressing itself as a whole in action. The person *himself* is invisible.... If the invisible side of people were discerned as easily as the visible side we would live in a *new humanity*. As we are we live in visible humanity, a humanity of appearances.... All our thoughts, emotions, feelings, imaginations, reveries, dreams, fantasies are invisible. All that belongs to our scheming, planning secrets, ambitions, all our hopes, fears, doubts, perplexities, all our affections, speculations, ponderings, vacuities, uncertainties, all our desires, longings, appetites, sensations, our

[3] *Living Time* (London, 1952), chap. 1. Quoted in Schumacher, *A Guide for the Perplexed*, p. 33.

> likes, dislikes, aversions, attractions, loves and hates – all are themselves invisible. They constitute "one's self." (italics added)

Nicoll insists that while all this may appear obvious, it is not at all overt:

> It is an extremely difficult thing to grasp.... We do not grasp that we are invisible. We do not realize that we are in a world of invisible people. We do not understand *that life before all other definitions of it, is a drama of the visible and the invisible.*[4] (italics added)

When I buy grain, my main interest is that it is alive and not dead. But that life I cannot see, touch, or smell. An unconscious cat, even though still alive, is not a real cat until it regains consciousness. This is what philosophers call "inner space." The matter itself is, however, mysterious. "Analyze, weigh and measure a tree as you please, observe its form and function, its genesis and the laws to which it is subject, still an acquaintance with its essence never comes about."[5] What smites us with total amazement is *not* what we grasp and are able to convey, but that what lies within our reach is beyond our grasp – not the quantitative aspect of nature, but something qualitative. Everything is more than the sum total of its parts. Man is aware of it, but it is beyond description or comprehension. Even the very act of thinking baffles thinking: the most incomprehensible fact is that man can comprehend altogether! That which man can apprehend man cannot comprehend. That which man takes account of, cannot be accounted for! "The search of reason ends at the shore of the known. We sail because our mind is like a fantastic sea-shell and when applying our ear to its lips, we hear a perpetual murmur

---

[4] Ibid.

[5] Ibid., p. 32.

from the wave beyond the shore."[6] And only through the awareness of this mystery does man start to live. Only then can he experience what real life is all about. The beginning of happiness lies in the understanding that life without the awareness of mystery is not worth living. Why? Because all life really starts in wonder and amazement! Being struck by the impenetrable mysterium of all being, the soul becomes reawakened. As if struck by fire, man is taken by a radical amazement. *This is the beginning of all genuine religion.* Because of man's astonishment with the world and himself, he recognizes the masterly hand of God. He ponders over the grandeur and sublimity of God. When seeing God as the foundation of all mystery, he starts to feel Him in his bones, in all that he does, feels, thinks and says! As has been said, the tendency to take everything for granted and the indifference to the sublime is the root of all irreligiosity. It is a way toward the secularization of the world. *Religion is a protest against taking things for granted.* It is the art of living in amazement.

Halacha

To be aware of the total mystery of all matter, to feel it, to breathe it, is obviously not an easy task. To become aware of the great secret behind all being is no doubt an art. How does man capture the notion of wonder and amazement and inject this into his very life? Some people sense these qualities at distant intervals, in extraordinary events, but can one capture it in every moment? This, the author would suggest, is only possible by capturing the mysterium and transforming it into a way of living. This is the purpose of the Halacha: to experience the mysterium in and through commonplace deeds. Halacha is the art of revealing the nonhuman side, the meta-human side, the divine dimension through the medium of every

[6] Avraham Yehoshua Heschel, *Man's Quest for God: Studies in Prayer and Symbolism* (New York: Charles Scribner's Sons, 1954), p. xiii.

human act. Halacha is there to teach us that our humanity is utterly inexplicable, that man should stand trembling before God. Judaism teaches that proper deeds lead to correct and true thinking. Deeds create mentality: the actual deed of killing creates a mentality to kill, the distribution of charity creates a mind-set to care for one's fellowman. Likewise, certain deeds have the power of making man walk through life in the awareness of the mysterium behind all human existence.

By giving deeds a certain direction, they become sensitized to the notion of mystery. By living Halacha we hold back and allow for a moment of reflection. It creates a mind-set not to take anything for granted but to become amazed by the very deed that follows. The dietary laws make man take notice, while eating, of the very wondrous existence of food, by making a *bracha* (blessing) on the miracle of eating. It stalls a deed, giving it an opportunity to transcend being a commonplace act and to become a higher deed. It causes a new profound reflection on life. Consequently, it provides for a different and more dignified way of living. It makes man take notice of his deeds and his life and ask, Why am I acting? What is the meaning of a human act and, therefore, of life?

What is there in the human deed that it should be the main carrier of this message? Is action the most important manifestation of human life? Why is philosophical reflection without the deed not good enough? Did not the Greeks contemplate the mystery of life without the Halacha? Does one really have to act so as to know? It is in the deed that man meets himself. In deeds man becomes aware of what his life is really all about: the power to harm, to wreck, and to destroy, but also the possibility of deriving joy and bestowing it upon others, of relieving or intensifying one's own and other people's tension. The deed shows man who he really is and not what he would like to be. Here his own self is exposed: what man does not dare to think, he shows in his deeds. The "real" heart of man is revealed in his deeds. Man may have lofty ideas but behave like a criminal. History teaches that noble ideas are no guarantee for noble deeds. And since God provided man with a world in which noble deeds are by far the most powerful ways to build and fashion this world, it is the deed that counts. No noble thought ever changed this world for the better if it did not become a noble deed. Metaphysics is not known for giving birth to noble deeds. But even when philosophical speculation would conduce man to act nobly, it would slowly evaporate into thin air if it did not go hand in hand with a firm and continuous commitment to a pragmatic deed. It is the deed that upholds the thought. It should be added that such an approach will only bear fruit when these deeds are constantly repeated. No human deed will leave its mark if done only once. To become effective it must grow into some kind of a habit as the result of its having rooted itself in the deep consciousness of man. Things continually done come to be done subconsciously. "Could the young but realize how soon they will become mere walking bundles of habits, they would give more heed to their conduct while in the plastic state. We are spinning our own fates, good or evil and never to be undone."[7] Habit is capitalized action. Habit becomes conscience. For this reason alone Judaism sees the deed as the key to teach man to recognize the mysterium. By way of rituals, blessings, and so on, often done in a habitual way and becoming second nature, man will subconsciously open himself up to the experience of amazement. Obviously this is no guarantee. Deeds, even when they carry the potential to reveal the mysterium, do not automatically result in a greater awareness. This will always depend on man's "conscious" awareness of what he is

---

[7] William James, *Principles of Psychology*, vol. 1 (New York: MacMillan and Co.).

doing. Only when man wills it to happen will the subconscious mind activate this potentiality.

What it does, however, is to lay the subconscious foundation of this awareness, so that if man should wish to capitalize on it, he may-thus enabling him to realize the wondrous aspect of human existence. In other words, a halachic life is not a guarantee that one will become consciously aware of the need to be amazed. One can live a halachic life without any notion of amazement. But what is important is that the Halacha gives man the option so that if he wants, he can achieve amazement, since he plants in his subconscious the seed for amazement. He turns his subconscious mind into an instrument that will take notice of the mysterium. It is also the uniqueness of "time" of which Halacha makes man aware. It is in time that man meets God. Every second that passes by is never to return. This makes time extremely precious. Consequently, it must be handled with the greatest of care. It teaches man that there are no insignificant moments or deeds. Whatever is done by man is to be done within the framework of an encounter with God. This requires that every deed be done with the awareness that one stands before the Lord of the universe and that every little matter, however unimportant in the eyes of man, counts. It is done in the presence of the King!

A New Awareness

The aim is to infuse purely subjective emotions, needs, and desires with a new awareness-one that otherwise is almost congenitally foreign to the entire component of the human personality. The religious system of Judaism, which disciplines the Jew in every situation all through life, establishes habitual patterns of bodily reaction and conduct that testify to an acute awareness of an order of reality that is not of the body. In that sense it liberates man from taking things for granted. This liberating act is a means, not a guarantee that it will result in a higher consciousness of amazement. When a Jew is overcome with nausea at the sight of nonkosher food, such a reaction is not natural; it is not in keeping with the laws of normal human experience. The reaction shows the awareness of some outside will that his personality has acquired. In a sense, the nausea reflects the partial transformation of the natural desire for food into the desire for that which is beyond man. It has often been said that Halacha requires mechanical, ritual performances. What is more important, the conscious worship of the mind or the quasi-automatic performances of the body? This is a question based on an utterly mistaken conception of the human personality. Man is made of body and soul. The body cannot worship consciously, and the mind is incapable of serving by way of ritual. Man is not only body or soul; he is the result of both and therefore in need of serving God in a way that corresponds to the body as well as to the soul, each according to its own nature. On the level of the soul, the relationship to God is spiritual and conscious, but there is no place for action. On the level of the body, there is no place for "conscious" worship. It can only be materialized into action. Only a combination can lead to an appropriate result. In the deed, the mitzvah is the union of the two. The mitzvah is never only thought, nor is it a mere reflex action. The mitzvah is a deed that is of the spirit and of the body at the same time. The subconscious condition toward the will of God and the mysterium tremendum is brought about by continuous conscious suggestion. Halacha is designed to make our lives compatible with our sense of the mysterium. What counts is not if it is compatible with common sense or the "obvious," but with that which is unspoken. What it wants to accomplish is to bring together the passing with the everlasting, the momentary with the eternal. And only through the human deed, transformed into a mitzvah, will it accomplish that task – to bring eternity into man's life, to redeem

God's power in every human experience, to discover divinity within man himself. Once it has done so, it is capable of turning every human deed into a mitzvah.

To Deserve

The fact that man is capable of acting, building, investigating, enjoying, and being aware that he can only take account of these faculties, but not account for them, confronts him with another inescapable question: Does he deserve these faculties? No normal man is without some concern for truth, beauty, or love. But can he make any claim on them? The shattering truth is that man does not deserve them, that he could not possibly deserve them. Nobody ever earned the right to love, to enjoy. No one ever earned these faculties through his or her talents or abilities. They are gifts, not rewards earned. It is as simple as that! Man experiences thousands of things and not one of them is really earned. This is most embarrassing! Man eats from Somebody's table with-out taking notice. Man's first concern should therefore be, Am I worthy? Do I deserve all this? How can I make myself worthy of all this? How will man respond to all these undeserved gifts? Without response there is no dignity! Love obligates, man must respond! Man needs to discharge his debts toward God. Only through that will he attain dignity. This is another aspect of halachic life. By living in accordance with Halacha as discussed above, man responds to God's ultimate gifts. He recognizes God's fingerprint in every and any matter. By redeeming God's power in this world, man sanctifies all his deeds; man becomes worthy of life!

Love becomes law in the life of the beloved. To be aware that man is the recipient of genuine love he imposes upon himself disciplines – the dos and the donts – that make him worthy of this love. This is, in fact, the hallmark of the mature human being. God's love becomes

God's commandment. Moral consequences follow, not without struggle and difficulties, not without the constant need to revise and rethink. With hard work, the heavens open and this awareness of the mystery becomes man's experience.